AN AMERICAN HARVEST

*Readings in
American
History*

Volume 1

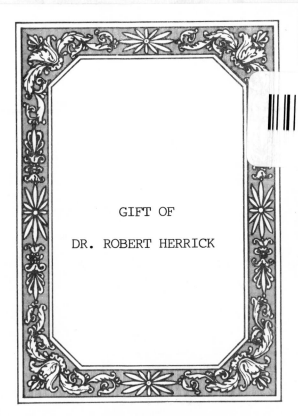

AN AMERICAN HARVEST

Readings in American History

Volume 1

J.R. Conlin
California State University, Chico

C. H. Peterson
California State University, Chico

Harcourt Brace Jovanovich, Publishers
San Diego   New York   Chicago   Atlanta   Washington, D.C.
London   Sydney   Toronto

ISBN: 0-15-502304-7
Library of Congress Catalog Card Number: 85-80083
Printed in the United States of America

to
G. D. Lillibridge,
generous friend

Preface

Montaigne said that historians spoil everything because "they chew our meat for us." He was right, of course. The task of historians is to study the documents—the primary sources, the meat of history—and to make of these a coherent, truthful representation of the past, as historians understand it, for those without the time or inclination to do so themselves.

Nowhere is the meat more thoroughly chewed than in survey courses in the history of the United States. How could it be otherwise? There are only a few weeks in every course, a few hundred pages in any textbook, in which to negotiate the complex experience of several hundred million Americans over nearly four centuries. Each instructor, each author must tell the story as swiftly and as simply as he or she can, wanly hoping that what is served up contains more than individual opinion.

It is only a minor improvement to supplement this fare by dragging in the "conflicting interpretations" of other historians. Two or three historians' truths undoubtedly make better grist for grinding than those of one. But if the historian's craft is worthwhile, why not present students with a few untouched portions on which to feast for themselves?

It is in the belief that the examination of primary sources can be a useful exercise in survey courses in American history that we have prepared *An American Harvest*. Although it can be used alone in courses organized around "problems" or "issues" and in classes that are blessedly small, we have arranged the reading material in ten sections corresponding to the periods into which American history is usually divided so that *An American Harvest* may be assigned in conjunction with any of the standard textbooks.

Within each section are five or six documents focusing on major questions of public policy. We have elected to include comparatively few documents, in part because of the crush of information and scarcity of time in survey courses and in part because this arrangement has permitted us to add more than the usual few words of sketchy introduction. In a foreword to each document we explain its historical context. In an afterword we comment on its subsequent history and significance. It bears emphasis that these auxiliary remarks are not pre-chewing. Their purpose is only to avoid the self-defeating consequences of presenting students with a document cold. They supply whatever information is required to permit students to understand the document in its own terms and to think about it for themselves.

In selecting the documents to be included in *An American Harvest* we have aimed to provide staple fare. Here are notable or representative documents that illuminate major questions of public policy in American history. Absent are essays on the social, cultural, religious, literary, or private lives of the American people, or of the many groups into which they have been divided, each with urgent concerns of its own. The broad questions of economic and social development included here are those which have engaged most Americans most of the time and around which they have organized their political efforts.

As editors our goal has been to provide readable texts useful to modern students. Therefore, especially in the earlier readings, we have modernized spelling, and here and there we have altered punctuation, whenever we believed the result would be a clearer version of the author's meaning. These are not, then, critical editions of the texts, especially since the limitations of space have prevented our using the whole of any but a few of them. But we have scrupulously respected the language of the originals. The words are the authors' own; difficult or obscure phrases are explained in the footnotes; omissions are indicated by ellipses; and, in the few cases where we have inserted a word, it is enclosed in brackets.

We thank Professor Jay Coughtry, University of Nevada, Las Vegas, for his helpful review of our manuscript.

J. C.
C. P.

Contents

PART 5   Sectionalism and Civil War 1831–1862

APPENDIX   The Charter Documents 1776–1971

AN
AMERICAN
HARVEST

Readings in
American
History

Volume 1

PART 1

❀ ❀ ❀

Colonial North America
1584–1755

1

Richard Hakluyt

❖ ❖ ❖

A Discourse Concerning Western Planting

1584

*D*uring the first 100 years after Columbus blundered upon the Americas, the English had very little share in them. Spain quickly seized all the easily extracted treasure of the continent, shipping the gold and silver of Peru and Mexico across the ocean to Seville. But even the *adelantados*, as the Spanish explorers of the sixteenth century were called, found little they could make use of in the rest of the vast New World. Sixteenth-century Europeans were able only to skim the cream away.

We must not exaggerate the technological capacity of early modern Europe. Although the mariners during the age of discovery accomplished wonderful feats, it was only by their astounding recklessness. The most seaworthy of Columbus' ships, the *Pinta*, was no bigger than a modern two-car garage, its equipment scarcely as sophisticated as that now owned by a suburban Boy Scout troop. In an age that has seen men go to the moon without loss of life, we shudder to think of Magellan, the greatest of the sixteenth-century navigators and the first to sail around the world. He left Seville in 1519 with 5 ships and 300 men; only one ship and 18 men ever

A DISCOURSE CONCERNING WESTERN PLANTING   From "A Discourse on Western Planting," ed. Charles Deane, Maine Historical Society, *Documentary History of the State of Maine* (Cambridge, 1877), II, 7–161.

saw home again. In the sixteenth century even the best-laid plans were grotesquely misinformed, and European adventurers often hurled themselves into the immense unknown with no greater control over their fate than daredevils shooting waterfalls in a barrel.

By the second half of the century English "sea-dogs," in the service of their canny spinster queen Elizabeth Tudor, were swarming across the Atlantic, lapping up any treasure spilt by the Spaniards. But this was only haphazard piracy. Before any but the crudest opportunities of the New World could be successfully exploited, the English, like other Europeans, needed to know much more about them.

It was their immense good fortune that printing was discovered about the same time as the New World itself. Instead of the new discoveries being shut up in dusty letter-files, the presses of Europe broadcast them to the world. In every country in Western Europe students set about the task of collecting and organizing a wealth of information gleaned from seafarers' descriptions of the new lands they had seen. Thus geography made its appearance as probably the first of the modern sciences.

In England the most influential of these armchair voyagers was the Elizabethan clergyman Richard Hakluyt. Like many other churchmen of his day, Hakluyt seems to have been little occupied by the cure of souls; instead his passion was the "new geography." He spent his life patiently collecting and collating any travel accounts that came to hand, combing them for whatever information they contained about the untapped economic opportunities of the planet. In 1589 he brought to press his great work, *The Principal Navigations, Voyages, and Discoveries of the English Nation*. It has been called the prose epic of early-modern England.

In 1584 Sir Walter Raleigh was hatching plans for a colony he hoped to establish on the North American coast, at about the 35th parallel, midway between Spanish Florida and earlier English failures in Newfoundland. The colony was to be called Virginia, in honor of the queen. In an effort to enlist her support, Raleigh persuaded Hakluyt to draft a lengthy memorandum, a portion of which follows. It was addressed to the crown, and it offered a summary of all the motives for English colonization in North America as they appeared to the best-informed Englishman of his generation.

I

❀ Seeing that the people of that part of America from 30 degrees in Florida northward unto 63 degrees (which is yet in no

Christian prince's actual possession) are idolaters; . . . and yet not-withstanding they are very easy to be persuaded, . . . it remaineth to be . . . considered by what means and by whom this most godly and Christian work may be performed of enlarging the glorious gospel of Christ, and reducing infinite multitudes of these simple people that are in error into the right and perfect way of their salvation. . . . Now the Kings and Queens of England have the name of Defenders of the Faith. By which title I think they are not only charged to maintain and patronize the faith of Christ, but also to enlarge and advance the same. Neither ought this to be their last work, but rather the principal and chief of all others, according to the commandment of our Saviour. . . . And this enterprise the princes of the [reformed] religion (among whom her Majesty is principal) ought the rather to take in hand, because the papists . . . have been the only converters of many millions of infidels to Christianity. . . .

IV

It is well worth the observation to see and consider what the like voyages of discovery and planting in the East and West Indies hath wrought in the kingdoms of Portingale[1] and Spain; both which realms, being of themselves poor and barren and hardly able to sustain their inhabitants, by . . . these, their new discoveries, . . . have so many honest ways to set them on work, as they rather want men than means to employ them. But we, for all the statutes that hitherto can be devised, and the sharp execution of the same in punishing idle and lazy persons, for want of sufficient occasion of honest employment, cannot deliver our commonwealth from mul-titudes of loiterers and idle vagabonds. Truth it is, that through our long peace and seldom sickness (two singular blessings of Almighty God), we are grown more populous than ever heretofore; so that now there are of every art and science so many, that they can hardly live one by another, nay rather they are ready to eat up one another. Yea many thousands of idle persons are within this realm, which,

---

[1]Portugal.

having no way to be set on work, . . . often fall to pilfering and thieving and other lewdness, whereby all the prisons of the land are daily pestered and stuffed full of them. . . .

Whereas if this voyage were put in execution, these petty thieves might be condemned for certain years in the western parts, especially in Newfoundland, in sawing and felling of timber for masts of ships, . . . in burning of the firs and pine trees to make pitch, tar, resin, and soap ashes; in beating and working of hemp for cordage; and, in the more southern parts, in setting them to work in mines of gold, silver, copper, lead, and iron; . . . in planting of sugar canes, as the Portingales have done in Madeira; in mainte-nance and increasing of silk worms for silk; . . . in gathering of cotton whereof there is plenty; . . . in dressing of vines whereof there is great abundance for wine; olives, whereof the soil is capable for oil; trees for oranges, lemons, almonds, figs, and other fruits, all which are found to grow there already; . . . in fishing, salting, and drying of ling, cod, salmon, herring. . . .

And seeing the savages of . . . Canada . . . are greatly delighted with any cap or garment made of coarse woolen cloth, their country being cold and sharp in the winter, it is manifest we shall find great utterance of our cloths, especially of our coarsest and basest; . . . whereby all occupations belonging to clothing and knitting shall be freshly set on work. . . .

In sum, this enterprise will minister matter for all sorts and states of men to work upon. . . .

V

We are moreover to understand that the savages of Florida are the Spaniard's mortal enemies, and will be ready to join with us against them. . . . And this is the greatest fear that the Spaniards have, to wit, our planting in those parts and joining with those savages, their neighbours, in Florida. . . . Which thing an English gentleman, Captain Moffett, who is now in France, told . . . that when he was in Spain, prisoner, not long since, he heard the treasurer of the West Indies say, that there was no such way to hinder his master, as to plant upon the coast near unto Florida. . . .

VII

And entering into the consideration of the way how this Philip[2] may be abased, I mean first to begin with the West Indies, as there to lay a chief foundation for his overthrow. And like as the foundation of the strongest hold undermined and removed, the mightiest and strongest walls fall flat to the earth; so this prince, spoiled or intercepted for a while of his treasure, occasion by lack of the same is given that all his territories in Europe out of Spain slide from him, and the Moors enter into Spain itself, and the people revolt in every foreign territory of his, and cut the throats of the proud, hateful Spaniards, their governours. . . . And this weighed, we are to know what Philip is in the West Indies; and that we be not abused with Spanish brags. . . . And therefore we are to understand that Philip rather governeth in the West Indies by opinion, than by might; for the small manred[3] of Spain, of itself being always at the best slenderly peopled, was never able to rule so many regions, or to keep in subjection such worlds of people as be there, were it not for the error of the Indian people, that . . . do imagine that Philip hath a thousand Spaniards for every single natural[4] subject that he hath there. . . . So as in truth the Spaniard is very weak there. . . .

If you touch him in the Indies, you touch the apple of his eye; for take away his treasure, which is *nervus belli*,[5] and which he hath almost out of his West Indies, his old bands of soldiers will soon be dissolved, his purposes defeated, his power and strength diminished, his pride abated, and his tyranny utterly suppressed. . . .

XIII

The manifold testimonies . . . of . . . Ribaut, . . . Verrazzano, . . . Gomez, . . . Coronado, . . . Cartier, . . . Corte Real, and others, which all were the discoverers of the coast and inland of America between 30 and 63 degrees, prove infallibly unto us that gold, silver, copper, pearls, precious stones, and turquoises, and emeralds, and

---

[2]Philip II, king of Spain 1556–98.
[3]Population of fighting men.
[4]Native.
[5]Sinews of war (a phrase from Machiavelli).

many other commodities, have been by them found in those regions. . . . Now the fifth part of all these aforenamed commodities cannot choose but amount to a great matter, being yearly reserved unto her Majesty. . . . What gains this imposition may turn unto the Crown of England in short time we may more than guess, having but an eye to the King of Spain's revenues, which he now hath out of all his dominions in all the West Indies. . . .

XX

A *brief* collection of certain reasons to induce her Majesty and the state to take in hand the western voyage and the planting there.

1. The soil yieldeth . . . all the several commodities of Europe, and of all kingdoms . . . and territories that England tradeth with, that by trade of merchandise cometh into this realm.
2. The passage thither and home is neither too long nor too short, but easy and to be made twice in the year.
3. The passage cutteth not near the trade of any prince, nor near any of their countries or territories, and is a safe passage, and not easy to be annoyed by prince or potentate whatsoever.
4. The passage is to be performed at all times of the year. . . .
6. This enterprise may stay the Spanish King from flowing over all the face of that waste firm[6] of America, if we seat and plant there in time. . . . How easy a matter may it be to this realm, swarming at this day with valiant youths, . . . to be lords of all those seas, and to spoil Philip's Indian navy, and to deprive him of yearly passage of his treasure into Europe, and consequently to abate the pride of Spain and of the supporter of the great Antichrist of Rome,[7] and to pull him down in equality to his neighbour princes, and consequently to

---

[6]Continent.
[7]The pope.

cut off the common mischiefs that come to all Europe by the peculiar abundance of his Indian treasure, and this without difficulty. . . .

7. This voyage, albeit it may be accomplished by bark or smallest pinnace, . . . yet . . . the merchant will not for profit's sake use it but by ships of great burden; so as this realm shall have by that means ships of great burden and of great strength for the defense of this realm. . . .

10. By this course . . . foreign princes' customs are avoided, and the foreign commodities cheaply purchased, to the common benefit of the people, and to the saving of great treasure in the realm. . . .

11. At the first traffic with the people of those parts, the subjects of this realm for many years shall change many cheap commodities of these parts for things of high value there not esteemed. . . .

13. By making of ships and by preparing of things for the same, . . . by planting of vines and olive trees, and by making of wine and oil, by husbandry, and by thousands of things there to be done, infinite numbers of the English nation may be set on work, to the unburdening of the realm with many that now live chargeable to the state at home. . . .

16. We shall by planting there enlarge the glory of the gospel, and from England plant sincere religion, and provide a safe and a sure place to receive people from all parts of the world that are forced to flee for the truth of God's word. . . .

18. The Spaniards govern in the Indies with all pride and tyranny; . . . so no doubt whensoever the Queen of England, a prince of such clemency, shall seat upon that firm of America, and shall be reported throughout all that tract to use the natural people[8] there with all humanity, courtesy, and freedom, they will yield themselves to her government, and revolt clean from the Spaniard. . . .

20. Many men of excellent wits and divers singular gifts,

---

[8]Indians.

overthrown by suertiship,[9] by sea, or by some folly of youth, that are not able to live in England, may there be raised again, and do their country a good service. . . .

21. Many soldiers and servitors, in the end of the wars, . . . may there be unladen, to the common profit and quiet of this realm. . . .

22. The fry[10] of the wandering beggars of England, that grow up idly, and hurtful and burdenous to this realm, may there be unladen, better bred up, and may people waste countries to the home and foreign benefit, and to their own more happy state.

❀ ❀ ❀

Raleigh's colony at Roanoke proved to be only another in a long string of English failures. The hundred luckless colonists deposited there in 1587 had vanished without trace by the time he tardily shipped new supplies to them four years later. Raleigh himself died on the headsman's block in 1618, having failed at virtually everything he had ever attempted. But both he and Hakluyt lived to see the first successful English colony founded at Jamestown in 1607. Hakluyt was involved in this project too, in an advisory role, although not entirely to the colony's benefit. His specifications were probably responsible for the unhappy decision to build Jamestown in a swamp. Few, if any, of his moneymaking ideas earned the return he had optimistically promised. For twenty years (until long after his own death) the colony suffered the stupefying loss of most of the money and lives invested there. But unlike Roanoke it was not abandoned. A generation of patriotic propaganda, to which Hakluyt had contributed more than his share, helped mobilize the national support necessary to see the colony through its difficult early years.

---

[9]Suit at law, civil litigation.
[10]Offspring.

2

John Winthrop
❖ ❖ ❖

A Model of Christian Charity
1630

The twenty thousand English
Puritans who emigrated to North America in the 1630s were, in their own
estimation, potentially the most significant group of human beings on
earth. They were Calvinists, members of perhaps the greatest international
revolutionary movement in European history before the rise of
Communism in the late nineteenth century. Like modern Communists,
Puritans believed the existing order was vicious, corrupt, and inevitably
doomed. Like them, most Puritans upheld rule by a single, authoritative
system of truth, or ideology, from which they tolerated no dissent. And like
Communists, they believed that they alone possessed the blueprint for the
future course of history. Puritans were "Reformed" Christians, not
Marxist-Leninists, but in retrospect we can see that their ideology, like
Communism in the present, helped to organize and discipline new,
revolutionary communities able to effect far-reaching changes in society.

In 1630 the immediate prospects for Calvinism in Europe were
darker than anyone then living could remember. Two years earlier the
French Calvinists had been crushed by Cardinal Richelieu at the terrible
siege of La Rochelle. In 1629, having rid his own vast empire of Calvinist
insurgents, the Hapsburg emperor had issued the Edict of Restitution,

A MODEL OF CHRISTIAN CHARITY   From "A Modell of Christian Charity," *Winthrop
Papers*, ed. Stewart Mitchell (Boston: Massachusetts Historical Society, 1931), II,
282–95.

returning to the Catholic Church all property taken by Protestants during the previous century of the Reformation in Central Europe. In England a new king, Charles I, had launched a severe repression against Puritan dissenters—Parliament had been dissolved, and the king's new archbishop, William Laud, vowed to harry Puritans out of the land. Thomas Hooker, the Puritan founder of Connecticut, expressed the mood of the Puritan community when he wrote, "God is going, His glory is departing, England hath seen her best days."

By the thousands then, beginning in 1630, English Puritans sold their goods, gathered their families, and departed too. In their eyes the Old World was doomed. They believed that they were watching the final days of the reign of the Antichrist, which prophecy foretold would occur just before the complete victory of Christ's Kingdom on earth. They saw themselves as a saving remnant, fleeing with the Gospel to the New World. Through their exemplary faithfulness they hoped that America might thus become the site of the glorious conclusion of human history. As the first contingent of Puritan emigrants crossed the Atlantic, their newly elected governor, John Winthrop, preached this lay sermon.

Christian Charity
A Model Hereof

❀ God Almighty in his most holy and wise providence[1] hath so disposed of the condition of mankind, as in all times some must be rich, some poor, some high and eminent in power and dignity, others mean and in subjection.

The Reason Hereof

1. Reason: First, to hold conformity with the rest of his works: being delighted to show forth the glory of his wisdom in the variety and difference of the creatures,[2] and the glory of his power, in

---

[1] In theology, God's government of the common affairs of this world, that is to say, of history.
[2] Created beings. Winthrop here argues by analogy to the plenitude of creation.

ordering all these differences for the preservation and good of the whole, and the glory of his greatness, that, as it is the glory of princes to have many officers, so this great King will have many stewards, counting himself more honoured in dispensing his gifts to man by man, than if he did it by his own immediate hand.

2. Reason: Secondly, that he might have the more occasion to manifest the work of his Spirit: first, upon the wicked in moderating and restraining them, so that the rich and mighty should not eat up the poor, nor the poor and despised rise up against their superiours and shake off their yoke; secondly, in the regenerate in exercising his graces in them: as in the great ones, their love, mercy, gentleness, temperance, etc., in the poor and inferiour sort, their faith, patience, obedience, etc.

3. Reason: Thirdly, that every man might have need of other, and from hence they might be all knit more nearly together in the bond of brotherly affection. From hence it appears plainly that no man is made more honourable than another, or more wealthy, etc., out of any particular and singular respect to himself, but for the glory of his Creator, and the common good of the creature, man. . . .

There are two rules whereby we are to walk one towards another—*justice* and *mercy*. . . . There is likewise a double law by which we are regulated in our conversation one towards another in both the former respects—the law of *nature* and the law of *grace*. . . . By the first of these laws, man as he was enabled so withall [is] commanded to love his neighbor as himself. Upon this ground stands all the precepts of the moral law, which concerns our dealings with men. To apply this to the works of mercy, this law requires two things: first, that every man afford his help to another in every want or distress; secondly, that he perform this out of the same affection which makes him careful of his own good. . . .

The law of grace, or the gospel, hath some difference from the former, as in these respects. First, the law of nature was given to man in the estate of innocency; this of the gospel in the estate of regeneracy. Secondly, the former propounds one man to another, as the same flesh and image of God; this as a brother in Christ also, and in the communion of the same spirit, and so teacheth us to put a difference between Christians and others. Do good to all, especially to the household of faith. Upon this ground the Israelites were to put a difference between the brethren [and] such as were strangers. . . .

It rests now to make some application of this discourse [to] the present design, which gave the occasion of writing of it. Herein are four things to be propounded: first the persons, secondly the work, thirdly the end, fourthly the means.

1. For the persons: We are a company professing ourselves fellow members of Christ, in which respect only though we were absent from each other many miles, and had our employments as far distant, yet we ought to account ourselves knit together by this bond of love, and live in the exercise of it, if we would have comfort of our being in Christ. . . .

2. For the work we have in hand: It is by a mutual consent through a special overruling providence, and a more than an ordinary approbation of the Churches of Christ, to seek out a place of cohabitation and consortship under a due form of government, both civil and ecclesiastical. In such cases as this the care of the public must oversway all private respects, by which not only conscience, but mere civil policy doth bind us; for it is a true rule that particular estates cannot subsist in the ruin of the public.

3. The end is to improve our lives, to do more service to the Lord, the comfort and increase of the body of Christ whereof we are members, that ourselves and posterity may be the better preserved from the common corruptions of this evil world to serve the Lord and work out our salvation under the power and purity of his holy ordinances.

4. For the means whereby this must be effected: They are twofold—a conformity with the work and end we aim at. These we see are extraordinary; therefore we must not content ourselves with usual ordinary means. Whatsoever we did or ought to have done when we lived in England, the same must we do and more also where we go. That which the most in their churches maintain as a truth in profession only, we must bring into familiar and constant practice, as in this duty of love. We must love brotherly without dissimulation; we must love one another with a pure heart fervently; we must bear one another's burthens; we must not look only on our own things, but also on the things of our bretheren; neither must we think that the Lord will bear with such failings at our hands as he doth from those among whom we have lived. . . .

Thus stands the cause between God and us: we are entered into covenant[3] with him for this work; we have taken out a commission; the Lord hath given us leave to draw our own articles; we have professed to enterprise these actions upon these and these ends; we

---

[3]A legal contract or promise. English Puritans introduced this terminology from the law into their theology, and argued that God dealt with man by mutually binding agreements.

have hereupon besought him of favour and blessing. Now if the Lord shall please to hear us, and bring us in peace to the place we desire, then hath he ratified this covenant and sealed our commission, [and] will expect a strict performance of the articles contained in it. But if we shall neglect the observation of these articles which are the ends we have propounded, and dissembling with our God, shall fall to embrace this present world and prosecute our carnal intentions seeking great things for ourselves and our posterity, the Lord will surely break out in wrath against us, be revenged of such a perjured people, and make us know the price of the breach of such a covenant.

Now the only way to avoid this shipwreck and to provide for our posterity is to follow the counsel of Micah: to do justly, to love mercy, to walk humbly with our God. For this end we must be knit together in this work as one man; we must entertain each other in brotherly affection; we must be willing to abridge ourselves of our superfluities for the supply of other's necessities; we must uphold a familiar commerce together in all meekness, gentleness, patience and liberality; we must delight in each other, make other's conditions our own, rejoice together, mourn together, labour and suffer together, always having before our eyes our commission, and community in the work, our community as members of the same body. So shall we keep the unity of the spirit in the bond of peace. The Lord will be our God and delight to dwell among us as his own people and will command a blessing upon us in all our ways, so that we shall see much more of his wisdom, power, goodness and truth than formerly we have been acquainted with. We shall find that the God of Israel is among us when ten of us shall be able to resist a thousand of our enemies, when he shall make us a praise and glory, that men shall say of succeeding plantations, "The Lord make it like that of New England."

For we must consider that we shall be as a city upon a hill. The eyes of all people are upon us. So that if we shall deal falsely with our God in this work we have undertaken, and so cause him to withdraw his present help from us, we shall be made a story and a byword through the world; we shall open the mouths of enemies to speak evil of the ways of God and all professors for God's sake; we shall shame the faces of many of God's worthy servants, and cause their prayers to be turned into curses upon us, 'til we be consumed out of the good land whither we are going.

And to shut up this discourse with that exhortation of Moses, that faithful servant of the Lord, in his last farewell to Israel: . . . Beloved, there is now set before us life and good, death and evil, in that we are commanded this day to love the Lord our God and to love one another, to walk in his ways and to keep his commandments and his ordinance and his laws and the articles of our covenant with him, that we may live and be multiplied, and that the Lord our God may bless us in the land whither we go to possess it. But if our hearts shall turn away so that we will not obey, but shall be seduced and worship . . . other gods, our pleasures and profits, and serve them, it is propounded unto us this day, we shall surely perish out of the good land whither we pass over this vast sea to possess it. Therefore, let us choose life, that we and our seed may live, by obeying his voice and cleaving to him. For he is our life and our prosperity.

❁ ❁ ❁

Puritanism in the English-speaking world did not outlast the seventeenth century. In England ten years of Puritan military dictatorship ended in 1660 with the restoration of the monarchy. British authorities stripped the "saints" of their power in Massachusetts in 1684, bringing an end to a "Millennium" which had lasted barely fifty years. During that half century, the Bible Commonwealth in New England displayed most of the unattractive features of all authoritarian states, including a stultifying compulsion toward conformity of thought and behavior, the cruel persecution of dissenters, and a general suppression of individual freedom.

But history is not simple. Winthrop's *Model of Christian Charity* illustrates the fact that the Puritan ideology cherished, in addition to its delusions, many ideals of present value. The belief that government should be limited by law, the duty of resistance to unjust authority, the desirability of government by the consent of the governed—these are ideals which passed from Puritanism into the modern political heritage of the Anglo-American world.

Even in the short run the achievements of Puritanism in New England were considerable. In the seventeenth century stern New England was one of the best governed, most orderly and well-disciplined communities in the Atlantic world. It was certainly the best settled group of colonies in British North America. And in time the sober, disciplined Yankees of New England made their region one of the very few in the world to participate fully in modern economic development.

What of the original dream? By the eighteenth century few believed any longer that the kingdom of Christ on earth had been inaugurated in Boston in 1630. But many Americans did believe that an Old World of injustice, oppression, and corruption had been left behind when the Atlantic was crossed, and that America offered a new beginning for humanity. When Thomas Jefferson called America "the world's best hope," his was a more secular version of John Winthrop's "city upon a hill."

3

Thomas Mun

❀ ❀ ❀

England's Treasure by Foreign Trade

1664

During the second half of the seventeenth century the ideological disputes which had agitated the Atlantic world for generations waned. The wars of dogma that had divided all of Europe into hostile Catholic and Protestant camps were submerged by the rise of a new and more compelling interest—trade. In the past Protestant England had struggled against Catholic Spain; now she made war on her sister Protestant republic Holland. "What matters this or that reason," said the Duke of Albemarle. "What we want is more of the trade that the Dutch now have."

The Atlantic world was in the midst of an extraordinary economic transformation. From time immemorial the subsistence economic tasks which had kept Europeans fed, clothed, and housed had been performed, not for the sake of profit, but because they were social duties to which each person had been assigned. In the critical matter of food production, for example, neither the farmer, the miller, nor the baker was thought actually to own the grain which passed through his hands. It was the responsibility of each to employ his particular skill in turn so that the community might eat bread. If anyone treated the grain as a commodity to be sold elsewhere

ENGLAND'S TREASURE BY FOREIGN TRADE   From *England's Treasure by Forraign Trade* (London: Thomas Clark, 1664), *passim*.

for a higher price (especially overseas), the community was outraged and the sheriff sometimes intervened.

Similarly, the wealth or "treasure" of a nation consisted of its stock of gold and silver. If any was spent for foreign goods, the nation was poorer. Loaning money out at interest was usury, an unneighborly practice condemned in the Bible, and merchants in general were poorly esteemed since no one could see that they produced anything at all. Most of these ancient attitudes, however, were permanently laid to rest in the English-speaking world during the seventeenth century. So great was the prosperity which the expansion of trade brought in its wake that the world was forced to revise its opinions and concede a new legitimacy to the activities of merchants.

In 1621 a grave economic depression aroused the old fears. Many blamed the depression on the East India Company for shipping silver to Asia to pay for trade goods. Thomas Mun, a rich London merchant, was one of the directors of the company. He wrote a reply in the company's defense which a few years later he refashioned into the elegant and coherent statement of economic theory which follows. It was published (after his death) in 1664.

I

The love and service of our country consisteth not so much in the knowledge of those duties which are to be performed by others, as in the skillful practice of that which is done by ourselves. And therefore (my son) it is ... fit that I say something of the merchant, which I hope in due time shall be thy vocation. Yet herein are my thoughts free from all ambition, although I rank thee in a place of so high estimation, for the merchant is worthily called the steward of the kingdom's stock, by way of commerce with other nations, a work of no less reputation than trust, which ought to be performed with great skill and conscience, that so the private gain may ever accompany the public good. ... The merchant['s] ... qualities ... in truth are such and so many, that I find no other profession which leadeth into more worldly knowledge. And it cannot be denied but that their sufficiency doth appear likewise in the excellent government of state at Venice, Lucca, Genoa, Florence, the Low Countries,[1] and divers other places of Christendom. And in those states also where they are least esteemed, yet is their skill and knowledge often used by those who sit in the highest places of authority. It is therefore an act beyond rashness in some, who do disenable their counsel and judgment, . . . making them uncapable of those ways and means which do either enrich or impoverish a commonwealth, when in truth this is only effected by the mystery of their trade, as I shall plainly show in that which followeth. . . .

II

Although a kingdom may be enriched by gifts received, or by purchase taken from some other nations, yet these are things uncertain and of small consideration when they happen. The ordinary means, therefore, to increase our wealth and treasure is by foreign trade, wherein we must ever observe this rule—to sell more to strangers[2] yearly than we consume of theirs in value. For suppose that when this kingdom is plentifully served with the cloth, lead, tin, iron, fish and other native commodities, we do yearly export the overplus to foreign countries to the value of twenty-two hundred thousand pounds, by which means we are enabled beyond the seas to buy and bring in foreign wares for our use and consumptions to the value of twenty hundred thousand pounds. By this order, duly kept in our trading, we may rest assured that the kingdom shall be enriched yearly two hundred thousand pounds, which must be brought to us in so much treasure, because that part of our stock which is not returned to us in wares must necessarily be brought home in treasure. . . .

III

The revenue or stock of a kingdom, by which it is provided of foreign wares, is either *natural* or *artificial*. The natural wealth is so much only as can be spared from our own use and necessities to be

---

[1]All places remarkable in early-modern Europe because they were ruled not by kings and landed aristocracies but by oligarchies of merchants.
[2]Foreigners.

exported unto strangers. The artificial consists in our manufactures and industrious trading with foreign commodities, concerning which I will set down such particulars as may serve for the cause we have in hand.

1. First, although this realm be already exceeding rich by nature, yet might it be much increased by laying the waste grounds (which are infinite) into such employments as . . . to supply ourselves and prevent the importation of hemp, flax, cordage, tobacco, and divers other things which we now fetch from strangers to our great impoverishing.

2. We may likewise diminish our importations, if we would soberly refrain from excessive consumption of foreign wares in our diet and raiment, with such often change of fashions as is used so much the more to increase the waste and change, which vices at this present are more notorious amongst us than in former ages. . . .

4. The value of our exportation likewise may be much advanced when we perform it ourselves in our own ships, for then we get not only the price of our wares as they are worth here, but also the merchants' gains, the charges of insurance, and freight to carry them beyond the seas. . . .

8. Also we ought to esteem and cherish those trades which we have in remote or far countries, for besides the increase of shipping and mariners thereby, the wares also sent thither and received from thence are far more profitable unto the kingdom than by our trades near at hand. . . .

11. It is needful also not to charge the native commodities with too great customs, lest by endearing them to the stranger's use, it hinder their vent.[3] And especially foreign wares brought in to be transported again should be favoured, for otherwise that manner of trading (so much importing the good of the commonwealth) cannot prosper nor subsist. But the consumption of such foreign wares in the realm may be the more charged, which will turn to the profit of the kingdom in the *balance of the trade*. . . .

IV

The exportation of our moneys in trade of merchandise is a means to increase our treasure. This position is so contrary to the common

---

[3]Sale.

opinion, that it will require many and strong arguments to prove it before it can be accepted of the multitude. . . . First, I will take that for granted which no man of judgment will deny, that we have no other means to get treasure but by foreign trade, for mines we have none which do afford it. And how this money is gotten in the managing of our said trade I have already showed: that it is done by making our commodities which are exported yearly to over-balance in value the foreign wares which we consume. So that it resteth only to show how our moneys may be added to our commodities, and being jointly exported may so much the more increase our treasure. . . . When we have prepared our exportation of wares, and sent out as much of everything as we can spare or vent abroad, . . . then we should add our money thereunto, . . . to enlarge our trade by enabling us to bring in more foreign wares, which being sent out again will in due time much increase our treasure. For although in this manner we do yearly multiply our importations to the maintenance of more shipping and mariners, improvement of his Majesty's customs and other benefits, yet our consumption of those foreign wares is no more than it was before. So that all the said increase of commodities brought in by the means of our ready money, [and] sent out as is afore written, doth in the end become an exportation unto us of a far greater value than our said moneys were. . . .

Thus may we plainly see, that when this weighty business is duly considered in his end, . . . it is found much contrary to that which most men esteem thereof, because they search no further than the beginning of the work. . . . For if we only behold the actions of the husbandman in the seed-time when he casteth away much good corn into the ground, we will rather accompt him a madman than a husbandman; but when we consider his labours in the harvest which is the end of his endeavours, we find the worth and plentiful increase of his actions.

VI

All the mines of gold and silver which are as yet discovered in the sundry places of the world, are not of so great value as those of the West Indies which are in the possession of the King of Spain, who thereby is enabled not only to keep in subjection many goodly states and provinces, . . . but also by a continual war taking his advantages doth still enlarge his dominions, ambitiously aiming at a monarchy by the power of his moneys, which are the very sinews of his strengths. . . .

[However], his wants [are] supplied both for war and peace in a plentiful manner from all the parts of Christendom, which are therefore partakers of his treasure by a necessity of commerce, wherein the Spanish policy hath ever endeavoured to prevent all other nations the most it could. For finding Spain to be too poor and barren to supply itself and the West Indies with those varieties of foreign wares whereof they stand in need, they knew well that when their native commodities come short to this purpose, their moneys must serve to make up the reckoning. . . .

[Formerly] they found an incredible advantage to add the traffic of the East Indies to the treasure of the West, for the last of these being employed in the first, they stored themselves infinitely with rich wares to barter with all the parts of Christendom for their commodities, and so furnishing their own necessities, prevented others [from] carrying away their moneys. . . . But now this great profit is failed, and the mischief removed by the English, Dutch, and others which partake in those East-India trades as ample as the Spanish subjects.

It is further to be considered, that besides the disability of the Spaniards by their native commodities to provide foreign wares for their necessities (whereby they are forced to supply the want with money), they have likewise that canker of war, which doth infinitely exhaust their treasure, and disperse it into Christendom even to their enemies, part by reprisal, but especially through a necessary maintenance of those armies which are composed of strangers, and lie so far remote, that they cannot feed, clothe, or otherwise provide them out of their own native means and provisions, but must receive this relief from other nations. . . .

XXI

The sum of all that hath been spoken, concerning the enriching of the kingdom, and the increase of our treasure by commerce with strangers, is briefly thus. . . . Let the merchants' exchange be at a high rate, or at a low rate; . . . let foreign princes enhance their coins, or debase their standards, and let his Majesty do the like; . . . let the Statute for Employments by Strangers stand in force or be repealed; let the mere exchanger do his worst; let princes oppress, lawyers extort, usurers bite, prodigals waste; and lastly let merchants carry out what money they shall have occasion to use in traffic. Yet all these actions can work no other effects in the course of trade than is declared in this discourse. For so much treasure only will be brought in or carried out of a commonwealth, as the foreign trade doth over- or under-balance in value. And this must come to pass by a necessity beyond all resistance. . . .

Behold then the true form and worth of foreign trade, which is, the great revenue of the King, the honour of the kingdom, the noble profession of the merchant, the school of our arts, the supply of our wants, the employment of our poor, the improvement of our lands, the nursery of our mariners, the walls of the kingdoms, the means of our treasure, the sinews of our wars, the terror of our enemies. For all which great and weighty reasons, do so many well governed states highly countenance the profession, and carefully cherish the action, not only with policy to increase it, but also with power to protect it from all foreign injuries: because they know it is a principal reason of state to maintain and defend that which doth support them and their estates.

❖ ❖ ❖

In 1776 the great champion of free trade, Adam Smith, identified Thomas Mun as the father of English "mercantilism," a word Smith coined to denote the restrictive economic policies of the British empire down to his own time. Mercantilism was premised on the balance-of-trade idea set forth by Mun. It was a system of economic nationalism in which the state took action to increase exports and promote the commerce of its own people by the exclusion of foreign merchants and manufactures. Mercantilism also encouraged colonies as a means to provide protected markets and proprietary sources of raw materials. The first of the Acts of Trade and Navigation which enforced these policies appeared in 1651. More than a century later American colonists were still complaining about the Navigation Acts on the eve of the American Revolution.

Adam Smith's celebrated criticisms, written when the economy of the Atlantic world was outgrowing the mercantilist system, should not obscure the fact that in its own day mercantilism had been genuinely innovative. As Mun's treatise shows, the distinctive feature of mercantilism was not its restrictiveness (which Smith deplored), but its claim that it was the activity of merchants which generated national wealth (a view Smith shared). Mercantilist policies attempted to increase the scope of that activity by protecting merchants from foreign competitors who (as in the case of the Dutch) sometimes had a head start.

Instead, if mercantilism is to be faulted it is for its neglect of domestic, as opposed to overseas, trade. Mercantilists like Mun correctly perceived the way in which exchanges between two countries with diverse products enriched both. But they failed to see (as Adam Smith did not) that internal exchanges also increased national wealth for much the same reason. Mercantilism was a product of the seventeenth century, when traditional moral attitudes and ancient economic habits still hindered the growth of a market economy at home. Overseas, where there were only colonists, foreigners, or natives to consider, merchants could innovate more freely. Hence it was foreign trade which first revealed to Europeans the secrets of modern economic growth.

4

William Penn

❁ ❁ ❁

Account of the Province of Pennsylvania

1681

*B*y the second half of the seventeenth century the circumstances of English colonization in North America had changed remarkably. The economic opportunities of the New World were no longer guesswork, as they had been in Richard Hakluyt's day. Instead the Chesapeake colonies had discovered the profitable cultivation of tobacco, colonies in the West Indies were learning to produce sugar, the middle regions of the mainland could profitably grow grain for the West Indies, and New Englanders could build and sail ships to carry all this trade back and forth across the ocean. The American colonist was no longer a reckless or doomed adventurer desperately trying to gain a foothold in the North American wilderness. Instead, after 1640, he was likely to be an Englishman of some means, eager to invest in a commerce which already flourished. New colonies were able to purchase ample provisions from their older neighbors until they became self-sustaining. The market economy had even solved the problem of procuring a laboring population. Impoverished Europeans could be purchased as indentured servants, or captive Africans could be bought for lifetime slaves.

As a consequence the method of colonization changed. The earliest colonies, like Virginia and Massachusetts, had been the work of public companies with hundreds of investors. Later the prosperous state of

ACCOUNT OF THE PROVINCE OF PENNSYLVANIA   From *Some Account of the Province of Pennsilvania in America* (London: Benjamin Clark, 1681), *passim.*

American trade and the relative ease of settlement made the founding of colonies by private persons an attractive proposition. Between 1632 and 1681 British authorities distributed most of what was left of North America among individual "proprietors" as rewards for public and political service and as inducements to overseas enterprise. New York, New Jersey, Pennsylvania, Delaware, Maryland, and North and South Carolina were all founded as proprietary colonies.

In two cases the ordinary motives of proprietary grants were supplemented by additional religious considerations. Lord Baltimore founded Maryland as a refuge for English Catholics, and Pennsylvania was opened up as a haven for persecuted Quakers. Unlike the Spanish or the French who insisted on religious uniformity among their colonists, it was the policy of the more commercial English to encourage the emigration of religious malcontents. In this way the colonial population could be built up rapidly while religious tensions were reduced at home. William Penn, to whom the princely grant of Pennsylvania was given in 1681, was the most socially prominent member of a despised sect that had caused continual religious disturbances since their organization in the 1650s by the visionary George Fox. In an apparent effort to rid his realm of the whole troublesome lot, Charles II gave Penn his grant. The same year Penn published the following promotional tract advertising the attractions of his new province. It was typical of the proprietary efforts of the time.

Since (by the good providence of God) a country in America is fallen to my lot, I thought it not less my duty than my honest interest to give some public notice of it to the world, that those of our own, or other nations, that are inclined to transport themselves or families beyond the seas, may find another country added to their choice, that if they shall happen to like the place, conditions, and constitutions (so far as the present infancy of things will allow us any prospect), they may, if they please, fix with me in the province hereafter described. But before I come to treat of my particular concernment, I shall take leave to say something of the benefit of plantations or colonies in general, to obviate a common objection.

Colonies then are the seeds of nations begun and nourished by the care of wise and populous countries, as conceiving them best for the increase of humane stock, and beneficial for commerce.

Some of the wisest men in history have justly taken their fame from this design and service. We read of the reputation given on this account to Moses, Joshua, and Caleb in Scripture-records; and what renown the Greek-story yields to Lycurgus, Theseus, and those Greeks that planted many parts of Asia. Nor is the Roman account wanting of instances to the credit of that people; they had a Romulus, a Numa Pompilius, and not only reduced, but moralized the manners of the nations they subjected, so that they may have been rather said to conquer their barbarity than them.

Nor did any of these ever dream it was the way of decreasing their people or wealth; for the cause of the decay of any of those states or empires was not their plantations, but their luxury and corruption of manners. . . . With justice therefore I deny the vulgar opinion against plantations, that they weaken England. They have manifestly enriched, and so strengthened her, which I briefly evidence thus.

1st. Those that go into a foreign plantation, their industry there is worth more than if they stayed at home, the product of their labour being in commodities of a superiour nature to those of this country. For instance, what is an improved acre in Jamaica or Barbados worth to an improved acre in England? We know 'tis three times the value, and the product of it comes for England, and is usually paid for in English growth and manufacture. Nay, Virginia shows that an ordinary industry in one man produces three thousand pound weight of tobacco and twenty barrels of corn[1] yearly: he feeds himself, and brings as much of commodity into England besides, as being returned in the growth and workmanship of this country, is much more than he could have spent here. . . .

2dly. More being produced and imported than we can spend here, we export it to other countries in Europe, which brings in money, or the growth of those countries, which is the same thing. And this is the advantage of the English merchants and seamen.

3dly. Such as could not only not marry here, but hardly live and allow themselves clothes, do marry there, and bestow thrice more in all necessaries and conveniencies (and not a little in ornamental things too) for themselves, their wives and children, both as to apparel and household stuff; which coming out of England, I say 'tis impossible that England should not be a considerable gainer.

Thus much to justify the credit and benefit of plantations; wherein I have not sought to speak my interest, but my judgment; and I dare venture the success of it with all sober and considering men. I shall now proceed to give some account of my own concern. . . .

---

[1]Grain.

I. Something of the Place

The place lies 600 miles nearer the sun than England, for . . . [it] begins at . . . about the latitude of Naples in Italy, or Montpellier in France. I shall say little in its praise, to excite desires in any, whatever I could truly write as to the soil, air and water. This shall satisfy me, that by the blessing of God, and the honesty and industry of man, it may be a good and fruitful land.

For navigation it is said to have two conveniencies; the one by lying ninescore miles upon Delaware River, . . . where a vessel of two hundred tuns may sail. . . . The other convenience is through Chesapeake Bay.

For timber and other wood there is variety for the use of man.

For fowl, fish, and wild deer, they are reported to be plentiful in those parts. Our English provision is likewise now to be had there at reasonable rates. The commodities that the country is thought to be capable of are silk, flax, hemp, wine, cider, woad, madder, licorice, tobacco, pot-ashes, and iron, and it does actually produce hides, tallow, pipe-staves,[2] beef, pork, sheep, wool, corn—as wheat, barley, rye—also furs, as your peltry, minks, raccoons, martens, and such like store of furs which is to be found among the Indians, that are profitable commodities in Europe.

The way of trading in those countries is thus: they send to the Southern plantations corn, beef, pork, fish and pipe-staves, and take their growth and bring for England. [They] return with English goods to their own country. Their furs they bring for England, and either sell them here, or carry them out again to other parts of Europe, where they will yield a better price. And for those that will follow merchandise and navigation there is conveniency, and timber sufficient for shipping.

II. The Constitutions

For the constitution of the country, the patent[3] shows, first, that the people and governour have a legislative power, so that no law can be made, nor money raised, but by the people's consent.

---

[2]Barrel staves. Cooperage was the largest manufacture in the colonies. The barrels were used to ship colonial produce overseas.

[3]The royal document granting the colony to Penn.

2dly. That the rights and freedoms of England (the best and largest in Europe) shall be in force there.

3dly. That making no law against allegiance (which should we, 'twere by the law of England void of itself that moment), we may enact what laws we please for the good prosperity and security of the said province.

4thly. That so soon as any are engaged with me, we shall begin a scheme or draught together, such as shall give ample testimony of my sincere inclinations to encourage planters, and settle a free, just and industrious colony there.

III. The Conditions

My conditions will relate to three sorts of people: 1st. those that will buy; 2dly. those that take up land upon rent; 3dly. servants. To the first, the shares I sell shall be certain as to number of acres; that is to say, every one shall contain five thousand acres, free from any Indian incumbrance, the price a hundred pounds, and for the quit rent[4] but one English shilling or the value of it yearly for a hundred acres; and the said quit rent not to begin to be paid 'til 1684. To the second sort, that take land upon rent, they shall have liberty so to do, paying yearly one penny per acre, not exceeding two hundred acres. To the third sort, to wit, servants that are carried over, fifty acres shall be allowed to the master for every head, and fifty acres to every servant when their time is expired. . . .

IV. What Persons Will Be Fit To Go

1st. Industrious husbandmen and day-labourers, that are hardly able (with extreme labour) to maintain their families and portion[5] their children.

2dly. Laborious handicrafts, especially carpenters, masons,

---

[4]A kind of feudal rent owed, in this case, to the lord proprietor of the colony.
[5]Provide with an inheritance or dowry.

smiths, weavers, tailors, tanners, shoemakers, shipwrights, etc., where they may be spared or are low in the world. And as they shall want no encouragement, so their labour is worth more there than here, and their provision cheaper.

3dly. A plantation seems a fit place for those ingenious spirits that being low in the world, are much clogged and oppressed about a livelihood, for the means of subsisting being easy there, they may have time and opportunity to gratify their inclinations, and thereby improve science and help nurseries of people.

4thly. A fourth sort of men to whom a plantation would be proper, takes in those that are younger brothers of small inheritances; yet because they would live in sight of their kindred in some proportion to their quality, and can't do it without a labour that looks like farming, their condition is too straight for them; and if married, their children are often too numerous for the estate, and are frequently bred up to no trades, but are a kind of hangers-on or retainers to the elder brother's table and charity. . . .

Lastly, there are another sort of persons, not only fit for, but necessary in plantations, and that is men of universal spirits, that have an eye to the good of posterity, and that both understand and delight to promote good discipline and just government among a plain and well-intending people. Such persons may find room in colonies for their good counsel and contrivance, who are shut out from being of much use or service to great nations under settled customs. These men deserve much esteem, and would be hearkened to. . . .

V. The Journey and Its Appurtenances

Next let us see, what is fit for the journey and place, . . . and what is to be expected and done there at first, that such as incline to go may not be to seek here, or brought under any disappointments there. . . . And because I know how much people are apt to fancy things beyond what they are, and that imaginations are great flatterers of the minds of men, to the end that none may delude themselves with an expectation of an immediate amendment of their conditions so soon as it shall please God they arrive there, I would have them understand, that they must look for a winter before a summer comes; and they must be willing to be two or three years without some of the conveniences they enjoy at home. And yet I must needs say that America is another thing than it was at the first plantation of Virginia and New England, for there is better accommodation, and English provisions are to be had at easier rates. . . .

The passage will come for masters and mistresses at most to six pounds a head, for servants five pounds a head, and for children under seven years of age fifty shillings, except they suck, then nothing.

Next being by the mercy of God safely arrived in September or October, two men may clear as much ground by spring (when they set the corn of that country) as will bring in that time twelve month forty barrels. . . . So that the first year they must buy corn, which is usually very plentiful. They may so soon as they come buy cows, more or less as they want; . . . these will quickly increase to a stock. So that after the first year, what with the poorer sort sometimes labouring to others, and the more able fishing, fowling, and sometime buying, they may do very well, 'til their own stocks are sufficient to supply them and their families.

❖ ❖ ❖

News of Penn's colony spread far, and Pennsylvania was an immediate success. By 1685 ninety ships had brought 8,000 settlers to the banks of the Delaware. It was a population buildup unmatched since the Puritan Great Migration of the 1630s. Some were Quakers just released from English jails. Others came from Wales, Ireland, Holland, and Germany. Almost overnight Philadelphia rivalled Boston as the metropolis of British North America.

As extraordinary as the growth of the new colony was the transformation that occurred among its Quaker settlers. Originally Quakers had been recruited from the fringes of English society. They had been petty shopkeepers, tradesmen, and mechanics, persons generally excluded from any of the cultural advantages enjoyed by the socially eminent. Fortified by ecstatic religious views, they had hurled themselves against virtually every aspect of established English society. Quaker militants had suffered floggings, fines, imprisonment, and death undaunted, some even carrying shrouds for their own burial. No wonder Charles II thought himself so well rid of them! The king may have supposed that any colony settled by Quakers would be a madhouse. Instead Pennsylvania turned out to be a colony distinguished for its sober, simple, prosperous, and peaceable ways. Behind this transformation lay the Quakers' great aptitude for and steady application to trade. Within a few decades Quakers had established themselves as some of the most successful merchants in Atlantic commerce. Like many after them, Quakers found that the new market economy offered ordinary but diligent persons opportunities to rise in the world denied them by traditional social arrangements. Indeed the fertile farmland of the Delaware Valley and Philadelphia's well-chosen commercial location gave eighteenth-century Pennsylvania the reputation of being "the best poor man's country in the world."

5

Benjamin Franklin

❖ ❖ ❖

Observations Concerning the Increase of Mankind
1755

*T*he object of European colonization in thinly inhabited North America was, by definition, to fill the country with settlers. Between 1700 and 1775 the population of the thirteen British colonies grew from 250,000 to 2,500,000—doubling in each 25 years. About two-sevenths of this increase resulted from the immigration into the colonies of 400,000 Europeans and 250,000 Africans. The rest was due to an extraordinarily high rate of natural increase.

In fact the American colonies were among the first regions in the world to enter what has sometimes been called the modern demographic age. Before the eighteenth century the population of the world was only an eighth its present size. Famine and epidemic disease had prevented any significant growth for many centuries. It is estimated that during the hundred years before 1750 the average rate of population increase in England was 0.5 percent annually. By contrast the natural rate of increase in England's thirteen American colonies was 2.5 percent a year.

A few comparisons will illustrate the human significance of these

OBSERVATIONS CONCERNING THE INCREASE OF MANKIND   In William Clarke, *Observations on the Late and Present Conduct of the French . . . in North America* (Boston: S. Kneeland, 1755).

numbers. In England before 1750 average life expectancy was not much above 30 years (roughly that of Haiti or India in the twentieth century). Among other causes, extremely high infant mortality shortened the average lifespan—200 dead out of every thousand births in normal times (in London only a third of children ever reached the age of 5). Overall the death rate ran about 30 per thousand population each year. (By contrast, the present rate in the United States is 9.)

Because fertile land had long been fully occupied in Western Europe, the living were discouraged from bearing more children than necessary to replace the dead. Only the more fortunate married, and they late in life. The average English bride was nearly 25, her husband almost 30. The average marriage produced four children and contributed to a birth rate of about 35 per thousand (again that of present-day India). A very high death rate and a birth rate not much greater were characteristics of pre-modern societies.

In the thirteen colonies, by contrast, economic opportunity invited a much higher reproductive rate while a lower incidence of epidemic disease reduced mortality. For example, one scholar has found that in the town of Andover, Massachusetts, at the beginning of the eighteenth century there was a birth rate of 50 per thousand and a death rate of 15 per thousand! Women married as young as 21 or 22, and the average family size was 8 children. Life expectancy in Andover was about 50 years.

Andover was an extreme case, but the indisputable growth in the population of the colonies requires there to have been a birth rate of 40–50 per thousand and a death rate of 15–25 per thousand in the eighteenth century. It was a forerunner of a transformation that would overtake the entire Atlantic world. One of the first to take note of the new development was the astute American observer Benjamin Franklin in the celebrated essay which follows.

✿ 1. Tables of the proportion of marriages to births, of deaths to births, of marriages to the number of inhabitants, etc., formed on observations made upon the bills of mortality, christenings, etc., of populous cities, will not suit countries; nor will tables formed on observations made on full settled old countries, as Europe, suit new countries, as America.

2. For people increase in proportion to the number of marriages, and that is greater in proportion to the ease and convenience of supporting a family. When families can be easily supported, more persons marry, and earlier in life.

3. In cities, where all trades, occupations and offices are full, many delay marrying till they can see how to bear the charges of a family, which charges are greater in cities, as luxury is more common. Many live single during life and continue servants to families, journeymen to trades, etc. Hence cities do not by natural generation supply themselves with inhabitants; the deaths are more than the births.

4. In countries full settled, the case must be nearly the same. All lands being occupied and improved to the heighth, those who cannot get land must labor for others who have it. When labourers are plenty, their wages will be low; by low wages a family is supported with difficulty. This difficulty deters many from marriage, who therefore long continue servants and single. Only as the cities take supplies of people from the country, and thereby make a little more room in the country, marriage is a little more encouraged there, and the births exceed the deaths.

5. Europe is generally full settled with husbandmen, manufacturers, etc., and therefore cannot now much increase in people. America is chiefly occupied by Indians, who subsist mostly by hunting. But as the hunter, of all men, requires the greatest quantity of land from whence to draw his subsistence (the husbandman subsisting on much less, the gardener on still less, and the manufacturer requiring least of all), the European found America as fully settled as it well could be by hunters. Yet these having large tracts, were easily prevailed on to part with portions of territory to the newcomers, who did not much interfere with the natives in hunting, and furnished them with many things they wanted.

6. Land being thus plenty in America, and so cheap as that a labouring man, that understands husbandry, can in a short time save money enough to purchase a piece of new land sufficient for a plantation whereon he may subsist a family, such are not afraid to marry. For if they even look far enough forward to consider how their children, when grown up, are to be provided for, they see that more land is to be had at rates equally easy, all circumstances considered.

7. Hence marriages in America are more general, and more generally early, than in Europe. And if it is reckoned there that there is but one marriage per annum among 100 persons, perhaps we may here reckon two. And if in Europe they have but four births to a marriage (many of their marriages being late), we may here reckon eight; of which, if one half grow up, and our marriages are made reckoning one with another at twenty years of age, our people must at least be doubled every twenty years.

8. But notwithstanding this increase, so vast is the territory of North America, that it will require many ages to settle it fully. And till it is fully settled, labour will never be cheap here, where no man continues long a labourer for others, but gets a plantation of his own, [and] no man continues long a journeyman to a trade, but goes among those new settlers, and sets up for himself, etc. Hence labour is no cheaper now in Pennsylvania than it was thirty years ago, though so many thousand labouring people have been imported. . . .

13. As the increase of people depends on the encourage-ment of marriages, the following things must diminish a nation, viz. . . . 3. Loss of trade. Manufacturers exported draw subsistence from foreign countries for numbers who are thereby enabled to marry and raise families. If the nation be deprived of any branch of trade, . . . it will also be soon deprived of so many people. 4. Loss of food. Suppose a nation has a fishery; . . . if another nation becomes master of the seas, and prevents the fishery, the people will diminish in proportion. . . . 5. Bad government and insecure property. Peo-ple not only leave such a country, and settling abroad incorporate with other nations, . . . but the industry of those that remain being discouraged, the quantity of subsistence in the country is lessened, and the support of a family becomes more difficult. So heavy taxes tend to diminish a people. 6. The introduction of slaves. The Ne-groes brought into the English sugar islands have greatly dimin-ished the whites there. The poor are by this means deprived of employment, while a few families acquire vast estates, which they spend on foreign luxuries. And educating their children in the habit of those luxuries, the same income is needed for the support of one that might have maintained 100. The whites who have slaves, not labouring, are enfeebled, and therefore not so generally pro-lific. The slaves being worked too hard and ill fed, their constitu-tions are broken, and the deaths among them are more than the births; so that a continual supply is needed from Africa. The North-ern colonies, having few slaves, increase in whites. . . .

14. Hence . . . the legislator that makes effectual laws for pro-moting of trade, increasing employment, improving land by more or better tillage, providing more food by fisheries, securing prop-erty, etc., and the man that invents new trades, arts or manufac-tures, or new improvements in husbandry, may be properly called fathers of their nation, as they are the cause of the generation of multitudes, by the encouragement they afford to marriage. . . .

19. The great increase of offspring in particular families is not always owing to greater fecundity of nature, but sometimes to

examples of industry in the heads, and industrious education; by which the children are enabled to provide better for themselves, and their marrying early is encouraged from the prospect of good subsistence. . . .

21. The importation of foreigners into a country that has as many inhabitants as the present employments and provisions for subsistence will bear, will be in the end no increase of people, unless the newcomers have more industry and frugality than the natives. And then they will provide more subsistence and increase in the country, but they will gradually eat the natives out. Nor is it necessary to bring in foreigners to fill up any occasional vacancy in a country, for such vacancy (if the laws are good) will soon be filled by natural generation. . . .

22. There is, in short, no bound to the prolific nature of plants or animals, but what is made by their crowding and interfering with each other's means of subsistence. Was the face of the earth vacant of other plants, it might be gradually sowed and overspread with one kind only, as for instance with fennel; and were it empty of other inhabitants, it might in a few ages be replenished from one nation only, as for instance with Englishmen. Thus there are supposed to be now upwards of one million English souls in North America (though 'tis thought scarce 80,000 have been brought over the sea), and yet perhaps there is not one the fewer in Britain, but rather many more, on account of the employment the colonies afford to manufacturers at home. This million, doubling suppose but once in 25 years, will in another century be more than the people of England, and the greatest number of Englishmen will be on this side the water. What an accession of power to the British Empire by sea as well as land! What increase of trade and navigation! . . .

23. And since detachments of English from Britain sent to America will have their places at home so soon supplied, and increase so largely here, why should the Palatine boors[1] be suffered to swarm into our settlements, and by herding together establish their language and manners to the exclusion of ours? Why should Pennsylvania, founded by the English, become a colony of aliens, who will shortly be so numerous as to Germanize us instead of our Anglifying them, and will never adopt our language or customs, any more than they can acquire our complexion?

24. Which leads me to add one remark: that the number of

---

[1] A German or Dutch word meaning peasant or smallholder. The Palatine Germans, from the Rhineland, first arrived in the colonies in 1711 as war refugees. In subsequent decades they and other Germans immigrated by the tens of thousands, most of them to Pennsylvania.

purely white people in the world is proportionably very small. All Africa is black or tawny. Asia chiefly tawny. America (exclusive of the newcomers) wholly so. And in Europe the Spaniards, Italians, French, Russians and Swedes are generally of what we call a swarthy complexion, as are the Germans also, the Saxons only excepted, who with the English make the principal body of white people on the face of the earth. I could wish their numbers were increased. And while we are, as I may call it, scouring our planet by clearing America of woods, and so making this side of our globe reflect a brighter light to the eyes of inhabitants in Mars or Venus, why should we, in the sight of superior beings, darken its people? Why increase the sons of Africa by planting them in America, where we have so fair an opportunity, by excluding all blacks and tawneys, of increasing the lovely white and red? But perhaps I am partial to the complexion of my country, for such kind of partiality is natural to mankind.

❊ ❊ ❊

Franklin took for granted that increased numbers were beneficial. Mercantilism taught that people were wealth, so no nation could have too many inhabitants. In 1798 Thomas Malthus (who had consulted Franklin's figures) challenged this view in a famous essay which argued that any increase in wealth will soon be gobbled up by a corresponding growth in population. Therefore, said Malthus, there can never be any permanent improvement in society. For reasons difficult to assign, Malthus' grim prediction failed to hold in Western Europe and North America. But the experience of many developing nations today shows that the danger is real.

Franklin's own misgivings concerned not the numbers of the American population but its mixed character. The ambitions of colonial proprietors and the policies of imperial officials led them to accept settlers willy-nilly wherever they could be found. By the middle of the eighteenth century the colonies were no longer wholly English. A quarter of the population was African. In Pennsylvania a third were Germans ("generally of the most ignorant, stupid sort," Franklin grumbled). Experience pointed to the disruptive effects upon communities of racial and ethnic minorities. Hence Franklin's fears.

In the case of Africans the tide was halted in Franklin's lifetime. The northern states, including Pennsylvania, abolished slavery when they won their independence after 1776, and even the southern states prohibited the further importation of Africans. However, the tide of European immigrants was running the other way. Throughout the Atlantic world governments abandoned restrictions that had always prevented movement across national frontiers. The century which followed Franklin's death became the only time in history when it was possible to travel virtually anywhere in the world without so much as a passport or visa. The fact soon set the United States awash in a flood of immigrants the size and diversity of which Franklin had never imagined.

Franklin's essay produced alarm of another kind in London where it was reprinted several times. In 1700 there had been 20 Englishmen for every colonist. By 1775 there would be only three. Imperial officials therefore concluded that unless measures were promptly taken to reduce the American giant to a more effective subordination than in the past, the empire would be lost. Their efforts to do so provoked the American Revolution.

PART 2

❀ ❀ ❀

The Revolution and the Constitution
1750–1787

1

Jonathan Mayhew

❈ ❈ ❈

Discourse Concerning Unlimited Submission
1750

*J*ohn Adams remarked that the American Revolution had occurred fifty years before 1776 in the minds and hearts of the people. It is true that the political ideas used by American revolutionaries to justify their break from Great Britain had been in their possession for many years beforehand. In the following sermon by the Reverend Jonathan Mayhew of Boston, we find a defense of the right of revolution and even language which anticipated that of the Declaration of Independence by a quarter century. The one thing lacking in 1750 was a pretext for revolt.

Mayhew's thought illustrates the liberalism which overtook the inherited religious culture of New England in the eighteenth century. Minister of Boston's fashionable West Church, Mayhew preached weekly to a congregation of bewigged and prosperous merchants to whom the Calvinist dogmas of John Winthrop's day had come to seem fantastic. Religious creeds, Mayhew declared, "are imperious and tyrannical, . . . an infringement upon those rights of conscience which ought to be sacred." Instead he advocated the "right and duty of private judgment"—the view that individuals should employ reason to settle religious questions for themselves.

DISCOURSE CONCERNING UNLIMITED SUBMISSION   From *A Discourse Concerning Unlimited Submission and Non-Resistance to the Higher Powers* (Boston: D. Fowle, 1750), *passim.*

In this sermon Mayhew took his text from Romans xiii, 1–7, a passage which begins, "Let every soul be subject unto the higher powers." His treatment of the text and his celebration of the example of Puritan ancestors who had overthrown Charles I illustrate the way in which biblical authority and the Puritan past could be invoked in New England, as they were during the Revolution, to reinforce the liberal political ideals of the eighteenth century.

God be thanked one may, in any part of the British dominions, speak freely (if a decent regard be paid to those in authority) both of government and religion, and even give some broad hints that he is engaged on the side of liberty, the Bible and common sense, in opposition to tyranny, priestcraft and nonsense, without being in danger either of the bastile or the inquisition; though there will always be some interested politicians, contracted bigots, and hypocritical zealots for a party, to take offense at such freedoms. Their censure is praise; their praise is infamy. A spirit of domination is always to be guarded against both in church and state, even in times of the greatest security, such as the present is amongst us. . . . Those nations who are now groaning under the iron scepter of tyranny, were once free. So they might, probably, have remained, by a seasonable precaution against despotic measures. . . . Tyranny brings ignorance and brutality along with it. It degrades men from their just rank into the class of brutes. It damps their spirits. It suppresses arts. It extinguishes every spark of noble ardor and generosity in the breasts of those who are enslaved by it. It makes naturally strong and great minds feeble and little, and triumphs over the ruins of virtue and humanity. This is true of tyranny in every shape. There can be nothing great and good where its influence reaches. For which reason it becomes every friend to truth and human kind, every lover of God and the Christian religion, to bear a part in opposing this hateful monster. It was a desire to contribute a mite towards carrying on a war against this common enemy that produced the following discourse. . . .

It is the duty of Christian magistrates to inform themselves what it is which their religion teaches concerning the nature and design of their office. And it is equally the duty of all Christian people to inform themselves what it is which their religion teaches concerning that subjection which they owe to the higher powers. It is for these reasons that I have attempted to examine into the scripture account of this matter, . . . not doubting but you will judge upon everything offered to your consideration with the same spirit of freedom and liberty with which it is spoken. . . .

The apostle's doctrine, in the passage thus explained, concerning the office of civil rulers, and the duty of subjects, may be summed up in the following observations, viz.

That the end of magistracy is the good of civil society, as such;

That civil rulers, as such, are the ordinance and ministers of God, it being by his permission and providence that any bear rule, and agreeable to his will that there should be some persons vested with authority in society, for the well-being of it; . . .

That disobedience to civil rulers in the due exercise of their authority is not merely a political sin, but an heinous offense against God and religion;

That the true ground and reason of our obligation to be subject to the higher powers is the usefulness of magistracy (when properly exercised) to human society, and its subserviency to the general welfare. . . .

There is one very important and interesting point which remains to be inquired into, namely the extent of that subjection to the higher powers which is here enjoined as a duty upon all Christians. Some have thought it warrantable and glorious to disobey the civil powers in certain circumstances, and in cases of very great and general oppression, when humble remonstrances fail of having any effect and when the public welfare cannot be otherwise provided for and secured, to rise unanimously even against the sovereign himself in order to redress their grievances—to vindicate their natural and legal rights, to break the yoke of tyranny and free themselves and posterity from inglorious servitude and ruin. It is upon this principle that many royal oppressors have been driven from their thrones into banishment and many slain by the hands of their subjects. It was upon this principle that Tarquin was expelled from Rome, and Julius Caesar, the conqueror of the world and the tyrant of his country, cut off in the senate house. It was upon this principle that King Charles I was beheaded before his own banqueting house. It was upon this principle that King James II was made to fly that country which he aimed at enslaving. And upon this principle was that revolution brought about, which has been so fruitful of happy consequences to Great Britain.

But, in opposition to this principle, it has often been asserted that the scripture . . . makes all resistance to princes a crime in any case whatsoever. If they turn tyrants and become the common oppressors of those whose welfare they ought to regard with a paternal affection, we must not pretend to right ourselves, unless it be by prayers and tears and humble entreaties. And if these methods fail of procuring redress, we must not have recourse to any other, but all suffer ourselves to be robbed and butchered at the pleasure of the Lord's annointed. . . . Now whether we are obliged to yield such an absolute submission to our prince, or whether disobedience and resistance may not be justifiable in some cases, . . . is an inquiry in which we are all concerned. . . .

If we attend to the nature of the argument with which the apostle here enforces the duty of submission to the higher powers, we shall find it to be such an one as concludes, not in favor of submission to all who bear the title of rulers in common, but only to those who actually perform the duty of rulers, by exercising a reasonable and just authority for the good of human society. . . . It is obvious . . . that the civil rulers whom the apostle here speaks of, and obedience to whom he presses upon Christians as a duty, are good rulers, such as are in the exercise of their office and power benefactors to society. . . . Thus it is said that they are not a terror to good works, but to the evil; that they are God's ministers for good. . . . And the apostle's argument for submission to rulers is wholly built and grounded upon a presumption that they do in fact answer this character, and is of no force at all upon supposition of the contrary. If rulers are a terror to good works, and not to the evil; if they are not ministers for good to society, but for evil and distress, by violence and oppression; if they execute wrath upon sober, peaceable persons who do their duty as members of society, and suffer rich and honourable knaves to escape with impunity; if instead of attending continually upon the good work of advancing the public welfare, they attend only upon the gratification of their own lust and pride and ambition, to the destruction of the public welfare; if this be the case, it is plain that the apostle's argument for submission does not reach them; they are not the same, but different persons from those whom he characterizes. . . . If those who bear the title of civil rulers do not perform the duty of civil rulers, but act directly counter to the sole end and design of their office, . . . they have not the least pretence to be honoured, obeyed and rewarded, according to the apostle's argument. . . . Rulers have no authority from God to do mischief. . . . It is blasphemy to call tyrants and oppressors God's ministers. They are more properly the messengers of Satan to buffet us. No rulers are properly God's ministers but such as are just, ruling in the fear of God. . . .

I now add, farther, that the apostle's argument is so far from proving it to be the duty of people to obey and submit to such rulers as act in contradiction to the public good, . . . that it proves the direct contrary. For, please to observe, that if the end of all civil government be the good of society, . . . and if the motive and argument for submission to government be taken from the apparent usefulness of civil authority, it follows that when no such good end can be answered by submission, there remains no argument or motive to enforce it. If instead of this good end's being brought about by submission, a contrary end is brought about, and the ruin and misery of society effected by it, here is a plain and positive reason against submission in all such cases, should they ever happen. And therefore, in such cases a regard to the public welfare ought to make us withhold from our rulers that obedience and subjection which it would otherwise be our duty to render to them.

If it be our duty, for example, to obey our king merely for this reason, that he rules for the public welfare, . . . it follows, by a parity of reason, that when he turns tyrant, and makes his subjects his prey to devour and to destroy instead of his charge to defend and cherish, we are bound to throw off our allegiance to him, and to resist; and that according to the tenor of the apostle's argument in this passage. . . . It is true the apostle puts no case of such a tyrannical prince; but by his grounding his argument for submission wholly upon the good of civil society, it is plain he implicitly authorizes, and even requires us to make resistance, whenever this shall be necessary to the public safety and happiness. . . .

For a nation thus abused to arise unanimously and to resist their prince, even to the dethroning him, is not criminal, but a reasonable way of vindicating their liberties and just rights. It is making use of the means, and the only means, which God has put into their power for mutual and self-defence. And it would be highly criminal in them not to make use of this means. It would be stupid tameness and unaccountable folly for whole nations to suffer one unreasonable, ambitious and cruel man to wanton and riot in their misery. And in such a case it would, of the two, be more rational to suppose that they that did not resist, than that they who did, would receive to themselves damnation.

And this naturally brings us to make some reflections upon the resistance which was made about a century since to that unhappy prince, King Charles I. . . . It was on account of King Charles's . . . assuming a power above the laws . . . and governing the greatest part of his time in the most arbitrary oppressive manner that that resistance was made to him which at length issued in the loss of his crown and of that head which was unworthy to wear it. . . . The nation had been patient under the oppressions of the crown . . . for a course of many years, and there was no rational hope of redress in any other way. Resistance was absolutely necessary in order to preserve the nation from slavery, misery and ruin. . . . God himself does not govern in an absolutely arbitrary and despotic manner. The power of this Almighty King . . . is limited by law; not indeed by Acts of Parliament, but by the eternal laws of truth, wisdom and equity, and the everlasting tables of right reason. . . . But King Charles sat himself up above all these, as much as he did above the written laws of the realm. . . . He lived a tyrant, and it was the oppression and violence of his reign that brought him to his untimely and violent end at the last. . . .

To conclude: let us all learn to be free and to be loyal. Let us not profess ourselves vassals to the lawless pleasure of any man on earth. But let us remember, at the same time, government is sacred and not to be trifled with. It is our happiness to live under the government of a prince who is satisfied with ruling according to the laws, as every other good prince will. We enjoy under his administration all the liberty that is proper and expedient for us. It becomes us, therefore, to be contented and dutiful subjects. Let us prize our freedom, but not use our liberty for a cloak of maliciousness. . . . For which reason I would exhort you to pay all due regard to the government over us, to the king and all in authority, and to lead a quiet and peaceable life. And while I am speaking of loyalty to our earthly prince, suffer me just to put you in mind to be loyal also to the supreme ruler of the universe, by whom kings reign and princes decree justice.

❂ ❂ ❂

Mayhew's discourse had been entirely academic in 1750, as his encomium to the "mild" government of George II shows. Indeed its only pretext had been the reactionary views of a handful of extremists in the Church of England—straw men if ever there were any. In 1765, however, history caught up with theory for Jonathan Mayhew. Confronted by the passage of the Stamp Act, Mayhew climbed the stairs of his pulpit to declaim against this new "great grievance." "If a nation is governed according to laws made by a single person, only for his own interest or pleasure, and one whom they do not choose or appoint to govern them," he cried, "such nation is in a state of slavery." The next day a mob destroyed the Boston mansion of Lieutenant Governor Thomas Hutchinson, stirred up, charged Mayhew's enemies, by "one of the most seditious sermons ever delivered." Mayhew was personally shocked and frightened by the imputed effect of his words. He died a year later, a believer in revolution conducted as it had been in 1647 by the duly constituted representatives of a nation, not by some horrid mob.

But the seditious words he had calmly penned in his study acquired a life of their own. Many years later John Adams recalled that Mayhew's *Discourse Concerning Unlimited Submission* had appeared the year before Adams entered Harvard. It was, he told Thomas Jefferson, "a tolerable catechism for the education of a boy of fourteen years of age. . . . I read it, till the substance of it was incorporated into my nature and indelibly engraved on my memory."

2

John Dickinson
❀ ❀ ❀

Letters from a Farmer in Pennsylvania
1768

*T*he best-known penman of the American cause before 1776 was John Dickinson, whose *Letters from a Pennsylvania Farmer* was written to protest the Townshend Duties of 1767. The title of Dickinson's book was more ingenious than ingenuous. Scarcely an ordinary farmer, he was one of the richest men in North America. Scion of a planter family, owning thousands of acres and scores of slaves in Maryland and Delaware, Dickinson was a successful Philadelphia attorney betrothed to one of the province's richest heiresses when he wrote the *Letters*. After their marriage they lived in great splendor on their "Fairhill" estate outside the city. Awestruck visitors described it as superior to any on the continent.

The *Letters* were in fact about property. They were the most widely read of all the defenses of the colonists' stubborn refusal between 1765 and 1775 to be taxed except by their own representatives. Dickinson's youthful training at the Inns of Court in London had impressed upon him a reverence for the legal principle that the people control the purse strings. He knew that Parliament's historic defense of this right had yielded the

LETTERS FROM A FARMER IN PENNSYLVANIA   From *Letters from a Farmer in Pennsylvania to the Inhabitants of the British Colonies* (Boston: John Mein, 1768), pp. 5–35.

freest government in Europe. Philosophy reinforced the lessons of history and the rules of the Common Law. John Locke taught that governments were formed solely to protect three basic rights enjoyed by mankind in nature—life, liberty, and property. The right to property, Locke thought, means nothing if not the right to exclusive possession: "For I have truly no property in that which another can by right take from me when he pleases, against my consent." Therefore any government which taxes unconsenting subjects annihilates property and contradicts its own founding purpose. Implicit in the cry "No taxation without representation" was the usually unargued assumption that the protection of private property is one of the few highest solemn duties of the state.

Letter I

My Dear Countrymen,

I am a farmer, settled after a variety of fortunes near the banks of the River Delaware in the province of Pennsylvania. I received a liberal education and have been engaged in the busy scenes of life, but am now convinced that a man may be as happy without bustle, as with it. My farm is small, my servants are few and good, I have a little money at interest. I wish for no more. My employment in my own affairs is easy, and with a contented, grateful mind I am completing the number of days allotted to me by divine goodness. . . .

From infancy I was taught to love humanity and liberty. . . . Benevolence towards mankind excites wishes for their welfare, and such wishes endear the means of fulfilling them. Those can be found in liberty alone, and therefore her sacred cause ought to be espoused by every man, on every occasion, to the utmost of his power. . . . These being my sentiments, I am encouraged to offer to you, my countrymen, my thoughts on some late transactions that in my opinion are of the utmost importance to you. Conscious of my defects, . . . I venture . . . to request the attention of the public, praying only for one thing—that is that these lines may be read with the same zeal for the happiness of British America with which they were wrote. . . .

Letter II

There is [a] late act of Parliament, which seems to me to be . . . destructive to the liberty of these colonies, . . . that is the act for granting the duties on paper, glass, etc. It appears to me to be unconstitutional.

The Parliament unquestionably possesses a legal authority to *regulate* the trade of Great Britain and all its colonies. Such an authority is essential to the relation between a mother country and its colonies and necessary for the common good of all. He who considers these provinces as states distinct from the British Empire has very slender notions of justice or of their interests. We are but parts of a whole; and therefore there must exist a power somewhere to preside, and preserve the connection in due order. This power is lodged in the Parliament, and we are as much dependent on Great Britain as a perfectly free people can be on another.

I have looked over every statute relating to these colonies, from their first settlement to this time; and I find every one of them founded on this principle till the Stamp-Act administration. All before are calculated to preserve or promote a mutually beneficial intercourse between the several constituent parts of the Empire. And though many of them imposed duties on trade, yet those duties were always imposed with design to restrain the commerce of one part that was injurious to another, and thus to promote the general welfare. . . . Never did the British Parliament, till the period above-mentioned, think of imposing duties in America *for the purpose of raising a revenue*. . . . This I call an innovation, and a most dangerous innovation.

It may perhaps be objected that Great Britain has a right to lay what duties she pleases upon her exports, and it makes no difference to us whether they are paid here or there. To this I answer, these colonies require many things for their use which the laws of Great Britain prohibit them from getting anywhere but from her. Such are paper and glass. That we may be legally bound to pay any general duties on these commodities, relative to the regulation of trade, is granted. But we being obliged by her laws to take them from Great Britain, any special duties imposed on their exportation to us only, with intention to raise a revenue from us only, are as much taxes upon us as those imposed by the Stamp Act. . . . It is nothing but the edition of a former book with a new title page, . . . and will be attended with the very same consequences to American liberty.

Some persons perhaps may say that this act lays us under no necessity to pay the duties imposed, because we may ourselves manufacture the articles on which they are laid. . . . But can any man acquainted with America believe this possible? I am told there are but two or three glasshouses on this continent, and but very few paper mills. And suppose more should be erected, a long course of years must elapse before they can be brought to perfection. This continent is a country of planters, farmers and fishermen, not of manufacturers. The difficulty of establishing particular manufactures in such a country is almost insuperable, for one manufacture is connected with others in such a manner that it may be said to be impossible to establish one or two, without establishing several others. . . . Inexpressible therefore must be our distresses in evading the late acts by the disuse of British paper and glass. . . .

Here then, let my countrymen rouse yourselves, and behold the ruin hanging over their heads. If they *once* admit that Great Britain may lay duties upon her exportations to us for the purpose of levying money on us only, she then will have nothing to do but to lay those duties on the articles which she prohibits us to manufacture, and the tragedy of American liberty is finished. . . . If Great Britain can order us to come to her for necessaries we want, and can order us to pay what taxes she pleases before we take them away, . . . we are as abject slaves as France and Poland can show in wooden shoes and with uncombed hair[1]. . . .

Letter III

Sorry I am to learn that there are some few persons, [who] shake their heads with solemn motion, and pretend to wonder what can be the meaning of these letters. . . . I will now tell the gentlemen. . . . The meaning of them is to convince the people of these colonies that they are at this moment exposed to the most imminent dangers, and to persuade them immediately, vigourously, and unanimously to exert themselves, in the most firm, but most peaceable manner for obtaining relief.

The cause of liberty is a cause of too much dignity to be sullied

---

[1]Dickinson adds in a footnote, "The peasants of France wear wooden shoes, and the vassals of Poland are remarkable for matted hair, which never can be combed."

by turbulence and tumult. It ought to be maintained in a manner suitable to her nature. . . . I hope, my dear countrymen, that you will in every colony be upon your guard against those who may at any time endeavour to stir you up, under pretences of patriotism, to any measures disrespectful to our sovereign and our mother country. Hot, rash, disorderly proceedings injure the reputation of a people as to wisdom, valour and virtue, without procuring them the least benefit. . . .

Every government, at some time or other, falls into wrong measures. They may proceed from mistake or passion. But every such measure does not dissolve the obligation between the governors and the governed. The mistake may be corrected, the passion may pass over. It is the duty of the governed to endeavour to rectify the mistake and appease the passion. They have not at first any other right than to represent their grievances and to pray for redress. . . .

To these reflections on this subject it remains to be added, and ought forever to be remembered, that resistance in the case of colonies against their mother country is extremely different from the resistance of a people against their prince. A nation may change their king, or race of kings, and retain their ancient form of government [and] be gainers by changing. Thus Great Britain, under the illustrious house of Brunswick[2] (a house that seems to flourish for the happiness of mankind), has found a felicity unknown in the reigns of the Stuarts. But if once we are separated from our mother country, what new form of government shall we accept, or when shall we find another Britain to supply our loss? Torn from the body to which we are united by religion, liberty, laws, affections, relations, language, and commerce, we must bleed at every vein.

In truth, the prosperity of these provinces is founded in their dependence on Great Britain; and when she returns to "her old good humour and old good nature," as Lord Clarendon expresses it, I hope they will always esteem it their duty and interest, as it most certainly will be, to promote her welfare by all the means in their power.

We cannot act with too much caution in our disputes. Anger produces anger, and differences that might be accommodated by kind and respectful behaviour may, by imprudence, be changed to an incurable rage. . . . We have an excellent prince in whose good

---

[2]The house of Hanover who, since the accession of George I in 1714, occupied the British throne.

dispositions towards us we may confide. We have a generous, sensible and humane nation to whom we may apply. They may be deceived; they may, by artful men, be provoked to anger against us; but I cannot yet believe they will be cruel or unjust, or that their anger will be implacable. Let us behave like dutiful children who have received unmerited blows from a beloved parent. Let us complain to our parents, but let our complaints speak at the same time the language of affliction and veneration.

❧ ❧ ❧

Dickinson had occupied advanced ground in 1768. He had swept aside the distinction between internal and external taxes, which some had drawn during the Stamp Act crisis, and declared that both violated colonial rights. In a few years, however, the forward rush of new men and events left him sadly to the rear. Radicals in the Continental Congress in turn scorned his own tenuous distinction between taxes for the purposes of revenue and taxes for the regulation of trade, the right to levy which he was ready to concede to Parliament. Even after the fighting had begun at Lexington and Bunker Hill, Dickinson refused to alter his views. "The first wish of my soul is for the liberty of America," he said. "The next is for reconciliation with Great Britain." In July, 1775, he drafted the Olive Branch petition to the King. Its tone of humble supplication enraged New Englanders suffering under the Coercive Acts. John Adams, who was as contemptuous of "the Farmer's" courage as he was envious of his fortune, maliciously blamed Dickinson's caution on the clamor of his womenfolk. "Johnny," his mother was supposed to have scolded him, "you will be hanged; your estate will be forfeited and confiscated; you will leave your excellent wife a widow, and your charming children orphans, beggars, and infamous." "Upon my soul," added Adams wickedly, "I pitied him." On July 2, 1776, when the vote was taken to adopt a declaration of independence, John Dickinson abstained.

3

Benjamin Franklin
❁ ❁ ❁

Rules by Which a Great Empire May Be Reduced to a Small One
1773

*B*enjamin Franklin was in London in 1773. He had lived in England for the previous nine years, and for fourteen of the nineteen years since 1754. Franklin mixed in as many of London's social circles as he had diverse interests. But much of his time was passed in the company of members of Parliament and other people involved in statecraft, for Franklin was a lobbyist for the Pennsylvania Assembly (and later, briefly, for the assemblies of Massachusetts and Georgia). He was also Deputy Postmaster General for all of British America. It was the highest imperial office to which any American ever rose.

Residence in England provided Franklin with a unique vantage from which to voice American concerns. An opponent of Parliament's attempts to tax Americans—what other position might a lobbyist for a colonial assembly take?—Franklin had nonetheless not been personally involved in the Stamp Act excitement and the boycott of British trade that followed the passage of the Townshend Acts. Consequently, he was able to communicate directly, even face to face with government officials, when tempers were

RULES BY WHICH A GREAT EMPIRE MAY BE REDUCED TO A SMALL ONE   First published in the London *Public Advertiser*, September 11, 1773. From *The Writings of Benjamin Franklin*, ed. Albert H. Smyth (New York: Macmillan, 1905–7), VI, 127–37.

hottest on both sides of the Atlantic. More important, Franklin assessed and criticized British policy from an imperial perspective. The interests of the empire were never prominent in the minds of Americans at home, but the London resident could and did examine the quarrel between the mother country and her daughters primarily in terms of how it affected the interests of Great Britain.

Two additional characteristics distinguish the two essays Franklin published in the London *Public Advertiser* in September, 1773, from the rest of the protest literature. First, "An Edict by the King of Prussia" and "Rules by Which a Great Empire May be Reduced to a Small One" are satirical. Irony, wit, and humor were singularly absent from the deadly earnest writings of John Dickinson, Samuel Adams, and the other colonial protesters.

Second, Franklin disdained the hair-splitting and ultimately moot distinctions between internal and external taxes, direct and indirect taxes, and even between virtual and no parliamentary representation that, in retrospect, lend a contrived, self-serving quality to the writings of many colonial protesters. From the British point of view, Franklin drove directly to the heart of the matter when he put Frederick the Great of Prussia in the position of addressing Britons as the British crown addressed Americans: arrogantly, as an imperial master. Frederick claimed this right because Britain was first settled by Germans, and because Frederick had fought to "defend" Britain in the Seven Year War.

Franklin was delighted when some British friends believed the Edict was genuine "till they had got half through it." It was especially effective satire because, although recently allied with Frederick, Britons regarded the Prussian king as a tyrant who had no respect for the liberties of his subjects. Franklin clearly conveyed the Americans' sense that, like the British, they too were part of a country sufficiently mature to take its place in the world. Also, in equating the colonies' relationship to Great Britian with Britain's relationship to Prussia, Franklin was slyly, but far from treasonously, introducing the conceivability of an independent America should Parliament persist in its folly.

"Rules By Which a Great Empire May be Reduced to a Small One" did not fool anyone until "they had got half through it." It represented a common kind of satirical essay that was relished by literate people of the late eighteenth century. Franklin wrote from the perspective of a person who wanted what virtually everyone else of that time, Briton and colonial alike, did not: the dissolution of the British empire.

❀ An ancient Sage boasted, that, tho' he could not fiddle, he knew how to make a *great city* of a *little one*. The science that I, a modern simpleton, am about to communicate, is the very reverse.

I address myself to all ministers who have the management of extensive dominions, which from their very greatness are become troublesome to govern. . . .

However peaceably your colonies have submitted to your government, shown their affection to your interests, and patiently borne their grievances; you are to *suppose* them always inclined to revolt, and treat them accordingly. Quarter troops among them, who by their insolence may *provoke* the rising of mobs, and by their bullets and bayonets *suppress* them. By this means, like the husband who uses his wife ill *from suspicion*, you may in time convert your *suspicions* into *realities*.

Remote provinces must have *Governors* and *Judges*, to represent the Royal Person, and execute everywhere the delegated parts of his office and authority. You ministers know, that much of the strength of government depends on the *opinion* of the people; and much of that opinion on the *choice of rulers* placed immediately over them. If you send them wise and good men for governors, who study the interest of the colonists, and advance their prosperity, they will think their King wise and good, and that he wishes the welfare of his subjects. If you send them learned and upright men for Judges, they will think him a lover of justice. This may attach your provinces more to his government. You are therefore to be careful whom you recommend for those offices. If you can find prodigals, who have ruined their fortunes, broken gamesters or stockjobbers, these may do well as *governors*; for they will probably be rapacious, and provoke the people by their extortions. Wrangling proctors[1] and pettifogging lawyers, too, are not amiss; for they will be forever disputing and quarrelling with their little parliaments. If withal they should be ignorant, wrongheaded, and insolent, so much the better. . . .

To make your taxes . . . odious, and . . . likely to procure resistance, send from the capital a board of officers to superintend the collection, composed of the most *indiscreet, ill-bred*, and *insolent* you can find. Let these have large salaries out of the extorted revenue, and live in open, grating luxury upon the sweat and blood of the industrious; whom they are to worry continually with groundless and expensive prosecutions before the abovementioned arbitrary revenue Judges; *all at the cost of the party prosecuted*, who' acquitted, because *the King is to pay no costs*. Let these men, *by your order*, be exempted from all the common taxes and burthens of the province, though they and their property are protected by its laws.

---

[1]Tax collectors.

If any revenue officers are *suspected* of the least tenderness for the people, discard them. If others are justly complained of, protect and reward them. If any of the under officers behave so as to provoke the people to drub them, promote those to better offices: this will encourage others to procure for themselves such profitable drubbings, by multiplying and enlarging such provocations, and *all will work towards the end you aim at.* . . .

If the parliaments of your provinces should dare to claim rights, or complain of your administration, order them to be harrassed with *repeated dissolutions.* If the same men are continually returned by new elections, adjourn their meetings to some country village, where they cannot be accommodated, and there keep them *during pleasure*; for this, you know, is your Prerogative; and an excellent one it is, as you may manage it to promote discontents among the people, diminish their respect, and *increase their disaffection.* . . .

If you are told of discontents in your colonies, never believe that they are general, or that you have given occasion for them; therefore do not think of applying any remedy, or of changing any offensive measure. Redress no grievance, lest they should be encouraged to demand the redress of some other grievance. Grant no request that is just and reasonable, lest they should make another that is unreasonable. Take all your informations of the state of the colonies from your Governors and officers in enmity with them; . . . act upon them as the clearest evidence; and believe nothing you hear from the friends of the people: suppose all *their* complaints to be invented and promoted by a few factious demagogues, whom if you could catch and hang, all would be quiet. Catch and hang a few of them accordingly; and the *blood of the Martyrs* shall *work miracles* in favor of your purpose. . . .

Send armies into their country under pretence of protecting the inhabitants; but, instead of garrisoning the forts on their frontiers with those troops, to prevent incursions, demolish those forts, and order the troops into the heart of the country, that the savages may be encouraged to attack the frontiers, and that the troops may be protected by the inhabitants. This will seem to proceed from your ill will or your ignorance, and contribute farther to produce and strengthen an opinion among them, *that you are no longer fit to govern them.*

❋ ❋ ❋

If the old saying is to be proved—that the pen is mightier than the sword—one would have to look somewhere besides "Rules By Which a Great Empire May Be Reduced to a Small One." Franklin's clever recipe for dismantling a cake was not even as mighty as the cudgels and grappling hooks of the Boston mob which, on December 16, 1773, clambered aboard British ships in Boston Harbor and dumped the cargos of tea into the black water. The "Boston Tea Party" so enraged George III, his prime minister Lord North, and their party in Parliament that they rushed through the "Coercive" or "Intolerable Acts" that led to the summoning of the First Continental Congress.

Franklin was therefore prophetic in "warning" the Crown not to regard colonial discontent as general, but to punish the "few factitious demagogues" who alone were responsible for the agitation. With the Coercive Acts, Lord North believed he could isolate the colony of Massachusetts, which he imagined was uniquely the cause of trouble; however, the Acts actually led to united colonial rebellion and, ultimately, to revolution.

When the news of the Boston Tea Party arrived in London, Franklin was already in trouble for an indiscretion in his service as Deputy Postmaster General. He was probably headed for dismissal anyway, but the events in Boston sealed his fate. He lost the postmastership.

Franklin remained in England through 1774, writing blistering attacks on British policy but also working, as were the members of the First Continental Congress, for a reconciliation. By 1775 he had given up. He returned to Philadelphia and was immediately elected as a delegate to the Second Continental Congress, which was far more inclined to independence than the First. He was a member of the committee that drafted the Declaration of Independence. After its author, Thomas Jefferson, Franklin was the chief contributor to the document which began the reduction of a great empire to a smaller one.

4

Thomas Paine

❋ ❋ ❋

Common Sense

1776

*A*ny authority which American colonists were still willing to permit Parliament to exercise over them vanished in 1775. That spring the war began in Massachusetts, and colonists read John Adams' essays which asserted that they were bound to the mother country not by Parliament, but only through the king. Because their assemblies had been dissolved by embattled royal governors, most colonies had created provisional governments which professed loyalty to the crown but ignored crown officials. London declared the colonies in "open and avowed rebellion" and dispatched an army of 20,000 troops. In December the Continental Congress replied, "What allegiance is it that we forget? Allegiance to Parliament? We never owed—we never owned it. Allegiance to our king? Our words have ever avowed it—our conduct has ever been consistent with it." The last remaining tie holding the empire together was loyalty to the king whose arms still hung above the door of the Pennsylvania statehouse where Congress sat. It was severed in January, 1776, by a pamphleteer who had arrived in the colonies only two years earlier, almost unknown, but, John Adams remarked, "with genius in his eyes."

Most American patriots, someone has said, were revolutionaries without being radicals. Thomas Paine was indisputably both. He had not been recruited from the gentry, but from the artisan class (his trade was ladies' corsets), a class which comprised perhaps half the population of a city like Philadelphia. Paine's political ideas were derived from socially

COMMON SENSE   From *Common Sense; Addressed to the Inhabitants of America* . . . (Philadelphia: W. and T. Bradford, 1776), *passim.*

obscure traditions which stretched back to the republicanism of the English Civil War among the working middle class. Literate, ambitious, skeptical, skilled, independent, but traditionally excluded from political affairs, this class found a spokesman in Paine, who raised his voice to introduce into the Revolution powerful egalitarian themes not previously addressed. In a world governed by kings, Paine preached republicanism, using direct language the impoliteness of which shocked his contemporaries. Paine estimated that *Common Sense* sold 150,000 copies. Those who could not buy it borrowed it; those who could not read heard it read aloud to them in the streets. Its proud author exclaimed that it was "the greatest sale that any performance ever had since the use of letters."

Of the origin and design of government in general. With concise remarks on the English constitution

Some writers have so confounded society with government, as to leave little or no distinction between them; whereas they are not only different, but have different origins. Society is produced by our wants, and government by our wickedness; the former promotes our happiness *positively* by uniting our affections, the latter *negatively* by restraining our vices. The one encourages intercourse, the other creates distinctions. The first is a patron, the last a punisher.

Society in every state is a blessing, but government even in its best state is but a necessary evil; in its worst state an intolerable one. . . . Government, like dress, is the badge of lost innocence. . . . For were the impulses of conscience clear, uniform, and irresistibly obeyed, man would need no other lawgiver; but that not being the case, he finds it necessary to surrender up a part of his property to furnish means for the protection of the rest. . . . Wherefore, security being the true design and end of government, it unanswerably follows, that whatever *form* thereof appears most likely to ensure it to us, with the least expense and greatest benefit, is preferable to all others. . . .

I draw my idea of the form of government from a principle in nature, which no art can overturn, viz. that the more simple anything is, the less liable it is to be disordered, and the easier repaired when disordered; and with this maxim in view, I offer a few remarks on the so much boasted constitution of England. That it was noble for the dark and slavish times in which it was erected, is granted. When the world was overrun with tyranny the least remove therefrom was a glorious rescue. But that it is imperfect, subject to convulsions, and incapable of producing what it seems to promise, is easily demonstrated. . . . I know it is difficult to get over local or long standing prejudices, yet if we will suffer ourselves to examine the component parts of the English constitution, we shall find them to be the base remains of two ancient tyrannies, compounded with some new republican materials.

First, the remains of monarchical tyranny in the person of the king.

Secondly, the remains of aristocratical tyranny in the persons of the peers.

Thirdly, the new republican materials in the persons of the commons, on whose virtue depends the freedom of England. . . .

The prejudice of Englishmen in favour of their own government by king, lords and commons, arises as much or more from national pride than reason. Individuals are undoubtedly safer in England than in some other countries, but the *will* of the king is as much the *law* of the land in Britain as in France, with this difference, that instead of proceeding directly from his mouth, it is handed to the people under the more formidable shape of an Act of Parliament. For the fate of Charles the First hath only made kings more subtle—not more just.

Wherefore, laying aside all national pride and prejudice, . . . the plain truth is, that it is wholly owing to the constitution of the people, and not to the constitution of the government, that the crown is not as oppressive in England as in Turkey.[1] . . .

Of monarchy and hereditary succession

Mankind being originally equals in the order of creation, the equality could only be destroyed by some subsequent circumstance. The distinctions of rich and poor may in a great measure be accounted

---

[1]Turkey was long a byword for oriental despotism.

for, and that without having recourse to the harsh, ill-sounding names of oppression and avarice. Oppression is often the *consequence*, but seldom or never the *means* of riches; and though avarice will preserve a man from being necessitously poor, it generally makes him too timorous to be wealthy.

But there is another and greater distinction, for which no truly natural or religious reason can be assigned, and that is, the distinction of men into *kings* and *subjects*. Male and female are the distinctions of nature, good and bad the distinctions of heaven; but how a race of men came into the world so exalted above the rest, and distinguished like some new species, is worth inquiring into, and whether they are the means of happiness or of misery to mankind. . . .

There is something exceedingly ridiculous in the composition of monarchy; it first excludes a man from the means of information, yet empowers him to act in cases where the highest judgment is required. The state of a king shuts him from the world, yet the business of a king requires him to know it thoroughly; wherefore the different parts, by unnaturally opposing and destroying each other, prove the whole character to be absurd and useless. . . .

To the evil of monarchy we have added that of hereditary succession; and as the first is a degradation and lessening of ourselves, so the second, claimed as a matter of right, is an insult and an imposition on posterity. For all men being originally equals, no one by birth could have a right to set up his own family in perpetual preference to all others forever. . . . One of the strongest natural proofs of the folly of hereditary right in kings is that nature disapproves it, otherwise she would not so frequently turn it into ridicule by giving mankind an *ass* for a *lion*. . . .

This is supposing the present race of kings in the world to have had an honorable origin; whereas it is more than probable, that could we take off the dark covering of antiquity, and trace them to their first rise, that we should find the first of them nothing better than the principle ruffian of some restless gang, whose savage manners or pre-eminence in subtilty obtained him the title of chief among plunderers. . . .

England, since the conquest,[2] hath known some few good monarchs, but groaned beneath a much larger number of bad ones; yet no man in his senses can say that their claim under William the Conqueror is a very honorable one. A French bastard landing with

---

[2]William, Duke of Normandy, conquered Saxon England in 1066, and his descendants still occupy the British throne.

an armed banditti, and establishing himself king of England against the consent of the natives, is in plain terms a very paltry rascally original. It certainly hath no divinity in it. . . .

In short, monarchy and succession have laid (not this or that kingdom only) but the world in blood and ashes. 'Tis a form of government which the word of God bears testimony against, and blood will attend to it. . . .

In England a king hath little more to do than to make war and give away places[3]; which in plain terms, is to impoverish the nation and set it together by the ears. A pretty business indeed for a man to be allowed eight hundred thousand sterling a year for, and worshipped into the bargain! Of more worth is one honest man to society and in the sight of God, than all the crowned ruffians that ever lived.

Thoughts on the present state of American affairs

In the following pages I offer nothing more than simple facts, plain arguments, and common sense. . . .

Volumes have been written on the subject of the struggle between England and America; . . . but all have been ineffectual, and the period of debate is closed. Arms, as the last resource, decide the contest; the appeal was the choice of the king, and the continent hath accepted the challenge. . . .

The sun never shined on a cause of greater worth. 'Tis not the affair of a city, a county, a province, or a kingdom, but of a continent—of at least one eighth part of the habitable globe. 'Tis not the concern of a day, a year, or an age; posterity are virtually involved in the contest, and will be more or less affected, even to the end of time, by the proceedings now. Now is the seed time of continental union, faith and honor. . . .

I have heard it asserted by some, that as America hath flourished under her former connection with Great Britain, that the same connection is necessary towards her future happiness. . . . Nothing can be more fallacious than this kind of argument. We may as well assert that because a child has thrived upon milk, that it is

---

[3]Government offices.

never to have meat. . . . But even this is admitting more than is true, for I answer roundly, that America would have flourished as much, and probably much more, had no European power had anything to do with her. The commerce, by which she hath enriched herself, are the necessaries of life, and will always have a market while eating is the custom of Europe.

But she has protected us, say some. . . . Alas, we have been long led away by ancient prejudices. . . . We have boasted the protection of Great Britain, without considering, that her motive was *interest* not *attachment*; that she did not protect us from our enemies on our account, but from her enemies on her own account, from those who had no quarrel with us on any other account, and who will always be our enemies on the same account. Let Britain waive her pretensions to the continent, or the continent throw off the dependence, and we should be at peace with France and Spain were they at war with Britain. . . .

But Britain is the parent country, say some. Then the more shame upon her conduct. Even brutes do not devour their young, nor savages make war upon their families. . . . But it happens not to be true, or only partly so. . . . Europe, and not England, is the parent country of America. This new world hath been the asylum for the persecuted lovers of civil and religious liberty from every part of Europe. Hither have they fled, not from the tender embraces of the mother, but from the cruelty of the monster; and it is so far true of England, that the same tyranny which drove the first emigrants from home, pursues their descendants still.

In this extensive quarter of the globe, we forget the narrow . . . extent of England, and carry our friendship on a large scale; we claim brotherhood with every European Christian, and triumph in the generosity of the sentiment. . . . What have we to do with setting the world at defiance? Our plan is commerce, and that, well attended to, will secure us the peace and friendship of all Europe. . . . As Europe is our market for trade, we ought to form no partial connection with any part of it. It is the true interest of America to steer clear of European contentions, which she never can do, while by her dependence on Britain, she is made the make-weight in the scale of British politics. . . .

As to government matters, it is not in the power of Britain to do this continent justice. The business of it will soon be too weighty and intricate to be managed . . . by a power so distant from us, and so very ignorant of us; for if they cannot conquer us, they cannot govern us. . . . Small islands not capable of protecting themselves are the proper objects for kingdoms to take under their care; but there is something very absurd, in supposing a continent to be perpetually governed by an island. In no instance hath nature made the satellite larger than its primary planet, and as England and America, with respect to each other, reverses the common order of nature, it is evident they belong to different systems. England to Europe, America to itself. . . .

O ye that love mankind! Ye that dare oppose, not only the tyranny, but the tyrant, stand forth! Every spot of the old world is overrun with oppression. Freedom hath been hunted round the globe. . . . Europe regards her like a stranger, and England hath given her warning to depart. O! receive the fugitive, and prepare in time an asylum for mankind.

✤ ✤ ✤

In a career which spanned an age of democratic revolutions, Paine's pen found employment on both sides of the Atlantic. "America has set you the example," he called to Europe in 1778, "and you may follow it and be free." He was in London to welcome the French Revolution when it broke out in 1789. Subsequently convicted of sedition by the English government, Paine went to France where he was elected a member of the National Convention which tried and executed Louis XVI. In 1793, during the campaign to "dechristianize" France, Paine wrote his last major pamphlet, vilifying Christianity. Its publication in America deeply offended both the pious and the politic among his former admirers. All his life Paine had been intemperate in his use of language and alcohol. Now the one cost him his public and the other his friends. "Citizen" Paine died in New York in 1809, the least mourned of American patriots.

It is worth remembering, however, that despite the controversy he generated, Paine advocated only middle-class values which most modern Americans take for granted. Before the industrial revolution, most of those who worked in the manufacturing trades were independent businessmen. The leather-aproned artisans and mechanics among whom Paine had been born included master tradesmen, who were the employers of their world, as well as wage-earning journeymen. Fiercely egalitarian, they disputed the pretensions of the titled and unfairly privileged, but they were intensely devoted to private property, business enterprise, and the interests of small, independent producers.

Unlike his friend Thomas Jefferson, who distrusted manufacturing, Paine foresaw limitless opportunities for democratic progress in the improvement of the mechanical arts. He was enthralled by the new mills, potteries, and foundries he saw in England. In the distinction between society and government which was basic to the argument of *Common Sense*, Paine never doubted that the free market was a natural and wholesome part of society itself.

5

James Madison
❖ ❖ ❖

The Federalist
1787

*T*he Revolution was both a war for
independence and a war against tyranny. It was a defense of inalienable
human rights against the British Crown's intolerable attempts to abridge
them. With this nobler cause uppermost in American minds during the
actual fighting, almost every state adopted a constitution that provided for
a weak governor, vested chief power in elected assemblies, and included a
bill of individual civil rights which government might not violate.

The Articles of Confederation, under which the thirteen states
regulated affairs among themselves and dealt with foreign powers, were
also designed to ward against the danger of a new tyranny. There was no
single, let alone strong, executive; no "monarch." Believing that republican
virtue and liberties were safe only in states of small extent, the authors of
the Articles ensured that each of the thirteen states was independent and
sovereign. The Confederation was not much more than an alliance.
Unanimous approval by all thirteen states, for example, was required
in order to levy a tax or to amend the Articles.

The weaknesses deliberately written into the Articles of
Confederation, and the frustration with what they saw as the
Confederation government's inability to take decisive action, offended
political leaders who dreamed of a great American *nation*. Men of this
ilk met in Philadelphia in 1787 and drafted the Constitution, which
dramatically swung the balance of power from the states to a new, more
centralized federal government.

THE FEDERALIST From *The Federalist: A Collection of Essays Written in Favour of the New
Constitution* (New York: J. and A. McLean, 1788), I, 79–86.

But this document could not become the new framework of government until the "Federalists" (as supporters of the new Constitution called themselves) won ratification of it by nine states. In particular, it was essential that the four largest states ratify it. Pennsylvania and Massachusetts did so by February, 1788. In Virginia and New York, however, opposition to the Constitution was better organized. The Anti-Federalists won considerable support with their argument that a strong central government was an invitation to the tyrannies that the Revolution had been fought against. To leading Federalists like James Madison of Virginia and Alexander Hamilton of New York, this argument was a smokescreen. The real reason for the Anti-Federalist opposition, they believed, was the fear of often venal provincial politicians that weaker state governments would mean less power for them and their petty self-interests.

Madison and Hamilton's distaste for provincialism had motivated them to work for a strong federal government in the first place. They had tried to sidestep the influence of provincial politicos by assigning ratification to specially elected conventions, rather than to existing state assemblies where their opponents were entrenched. Despite both men's considerable suspicion of democracy, they appealed to "We, the people" of New York and Virginia rather than to state leaders.

Their appeal took the form of eighty-four commentaries criticizing the Articles of Confederation and explaining why a stronger federal government was necessary. These were first published in New York newspapers and copied in Virginia. In book form, the essays are known as *The Federalist* and are considered some of the most masterful treatises in the history of political philosophy. Historian Garry Wills has pointed out the extraordinary intellectual energy that went into them. For six months, under the pen name of "Publius," Madison and Hamilton turned out "an average of a thousand well-chosen words every day." Wills has said, "It is enough to make all other writers on politics despair." In the later Federalist Papers, Madison and Hamilton analyzed each article of the new Constitution, explaining just how the new form of government would work. In the first thirty-six essays, they were more argumentative. They detailed the failings of the Articles and bluntly answered the Anti-Federalist objections to the Constitution by citing historical examples. One of the Anti-Federalists' strong points was the widespread belief that liberties were safe only in small republics, like the thirteen states or the city states of ancient Greece. Only in small republics could all citizens keep a close, personal watch on the operations of government. In "Federalist No. 18," Madison and Hamilton argued that the city states of Greece had eventually fallen to tyranny precisely *because* they were small, weak, and unable to unite. In "Federalist No. 14," reprinted here in part, Madison again undercut the Anti-Federalist argument by showing it applied to democracies and not to representative republics such as the Constitution proposed.

No. XIV

To the People of the State of New York:

We have seen the necessity of the Union, as our bulwark against foreign danger, as the conservator of peace among ourselves, as the guardian of our commerce and other common interests, as the only substitute for those military establishments which have subverted the liberties of the Old World, and as the proper antidote for the diseases of faction, which have proved fatal to other popular governments, and of which alarming symptoms have been betrayed by our own. All that remains, within this branch of our inquiries, is to take notice of an objection that may be drawn from the great extent of country which the Union embraces. . . .

[The objection] which limits republican government to a narrow district . . . seems to owe its rise and prevalence chiefly to the confounding[1] of a republic with a democracy, applying to the former reasoning drawn from the nature of the latter. The true distinction between these forms was also adverted to on a former occasion. It is, that in a democracy, the people meet and exercise the government in person; in a republic, they assemble and administer it by their representatives and agents. A democracy, consequently, will be confined to a small spot. A republic may be extended over a large region. . . .

As the natural limit of a democracy is that distance from the central point which will just permit the most remote citizens to assemble as often as their public functions demand, and will include no greater number than can join in these functions; so the natural limit of a republic is that distance from the centre which will barely allow the representatives to meet as often as may be necessary for the administration of public affairs. Can it be said that the limits of the United States exceed this distance? It will not be said by those who recollect that the Atlantic coast is the longest side of the Union, that during the term of thirteen years, the representatives of the States have been almost continually assembled, and that the members from the most distant States are not chargeable with greater intermissions of attendance than those from the States in the neighborhood of Congress. . . . We find that in Great Britain, inferior as it may be in size, the representatives of the northern extremity of

---

[1]Confusing.

the island have as far to travel to the national council as will be required of those of the most remote parts of the Union.

Favorable as this view of the subject may be, some observations remain which will place it in a light still more satisfactory.

In the first place it is to be remembered that the general government is not to be charged with the whole power of making and administering laws. Its jurisdiction is limited to certain enumerated objects, which concern all the members of the republic, but which are not to be attained by the separate provisions of any. The subordinate governments, which can extend their care to all those other subjects which can be separately provided for, will retain their due authority and activity. . . .

A second observation to be made is that the immediate object of the federal Constitution is to secure the union of the thirteen primitive States, which we know to be practicable; and to add to them such other States as may arise in their own bosoms, or in their neighborhoods, which we cannot doubt to be equally practicable. The arrangements that may be necessary for those angles and fractions of our territory which lie on our northwestern frontier, must be left to those whom further discoveries and experience will render more equal to the task.

Let it be remarked, in the third place, that the intercourse throughout the Union will be facilitated by new improvements. Roads will everywhere be shortened, and kept in better order; accommodations for travelers will be multiplied and meliorated; an interior navigation on our eastern side will be opened throughout, or nearly throughout, the whole extent of the thirteen States. The communication between the Western and Atlantic districts, and between different parts of each, will be rendered more and more easy by those numerous canals with which the beneficence of nature has intersected our country, and which art finds it so little difficult to connect and complete. . . .

I submit to you, my fellow-citizens, these considerations, in full confidence that the good sense which has so often marked your decisions will allow them their due weight and effect; and that you will never suffer difficulties, however formidable in appearance, or however fashionable the error on which they may be founded, to drive you into the gloomy and perilous scene into which the advocates for disunion would conduct you. Hearken not to the unnatural voice which tells you that the people of America, knit together as they are by so many cords of affection, can no longer live together as members of the same family; can no longer continue the mutual guardians of their mutual happiness; can no longer be fellow-citizens of one great, respectable, and flourishing empire. Hearken not to the voice which petulantly tells you that the form of government recommended for your adoption is a novelty in the political world; that it has never yet had a place in the theories of the wildest projectors; that it rashly attempts what it is impossible to accomplish. No, my countrymen, shut your ears against this unhallowed language. Shut your hearts against the poison which it conveys; the kindred blood which flows in the veins of American citizens, the mingled blood which they have shed in defense of their sacred rights, consecrate their Union, and excite horror at the idea of their becoming aliens, rivals, enemies. And if novelties are to be shunned, believe me, the most alarming of all novelties, the most wild of all projects, the most rash of all attempts, is that of rendering us in pieces, in order to preserve our liberties and promote our happiness. But why is the experiment of an extended republic to be rejected, merely because it may comprise what is new? Is it not the glory of the People of America, that, whilst they have paid a decent regard to the opinions of former times and other nations, they have not suffered a blind veneration for antiquity, for custom, or for names, to overrule the suggestions of their own good sense, the knowledge of their own situation, and the lessons of their own experience? To this manly spirit, posterity will be indebted for the possession, and the world for the example, of the numerous innovations displayed on the American theatre, in favor of private rights and public happiness. Had no important step been taken by the leaders of the Revolution for which a precedent could not be discovered, no government established of which an exact model did not present itself, the people of the United States might, at this moment have been numbered among the melancholy victims of misguided councils, must at best have been laboring under the weight of some of those forms which have crushed the liberties of the rest of mankind. Happily for America, happily, we trust, for the whole human race, they pursued a new and more noble course. They accomplished a revolution which has no parallel in the annals of human society. They reared the fabrics of governments which have no model on the face of the globe. They formed the design of a great Confederacy, which it is incumbent on their successors to improve and perpetuate. If their works betray imperfections, we wonder at the fewness of them. If they erred most in the structure of the Union, this was the work most difficult to be executed; this is the work which has been new modelled by the act of your convention, and it is that act on which you are now to deliberate and to decide.

PUBLIUS

❉ ❉ ❉

Despite what Garry Wills calls the "overkill" represented by *The Federalist* in the great debate (no Anti-Federalist treatise could hold a candle to it), the ratification convention in New York seemed certain to reject the Constitution as late as July 1788. Then, news arrived that Virginia had become the tenth state to ratify it. There, as in Pennsylvania and Massachusetts, more than a little political machination was involved in securing ratification. Nevertheless, the vote was significant because Virginia rivaled Massachusetts in historical prestige and was the largest of the thirteen states.

Fear of the possible disadvantages of being left out and the implied promise that New York City would be the first national capital probably had more influence on the New York delegates than did the Federalist Papers. In any case, New York fell into line on July 26. George Washington was inaugurated President the next spring. He named Alexander Hamilton his Secretary of the Treasury. James Madison sat in Congress as the first Speaker of the House of Representatives. John Jay, who had written three of the Federalist Papers, was the first Chief Justice of the Supreme Court.

PART 3

Federalism and Republicanism
1785–1823

1

Thomas Jefferson

❁ ❁ ❁

Notes on the State of Virginia
1785

*T*he wealth of nations, Adam Smith
helped the eighteenth century to see for the first time, is not measured
by foreign trade surpluses, as mercantilists had believed, but by the
production of "all the necessaries and conveniences of life . . . [in]
proportion to the number of those who are to consume it"—or, as we say
today, *per capita* GNP. Measured this way, Britain was the richest nation in
the world during Smith's time, and British North America was not far
behind. British prosperity, however, depended on the growth of
manufacturing. By 1811 only a third of English families still made their
livelihood through agriculture. In the United States, on the other hand,
farmers still constituted at least 90 percent of the population at the close
of the Revolution. The wonderful prosperity of the American colonies
had been so wholly the result of agriculture that Smith recommended the
United States continue to pursue a more or less strictly agricultural career.
Behind his advice lay a fundamental uncertainty in the eighteenth century
whether agriculture or manufacturing was inherently the more productive
occupation.

Agriculture found its greatest American advocate in Thomas

NOTES ON THE STATE OF VIRGINIA   From *Notes on the State of Virginia* (Philadelphia:
Prichard and Hall, 1788), pp. 40, 87–88, 174–78.

Jefferson, whose esteem for the land had many sources. He was himself a Virginia farmer. Classical authors, on whom he doted, taught him, in Cicero's words, that "Nothing is better than agriculture, nor more bountiful." Moreover, eighteenth-century political philosophy identified the independent landowner as the least corruptible of all citizens. At bottom, however, the question was an economic one, and Jefferson's views most closely resembled those of the eighteenth-century French economists called *physiocrats*.

The word "physiocracy" means "the rule of nature," and it was the physiocrats who first coined the phrase "laissez faire" to mean the absence of government interference in the natural workings of the economy. Their most notable doctrine, however, was that agriculture is the sole source of wealth. Nature, they said, cooperates with the farmer alone to give a yield superior to the cost of his labor or subsistence. The single seed which when sown yields a hundredfold illustrates a kind of natural generosity unique in the economic world. The manufacturing and trading classes, on the other hand, are "sterile." They produce goods only precisely equivalent in value to the cost of their labor, or subsistence consumption, leaving no net gain. Worse still are the "disposable" classes, those who provide only services— soldiers, priests, physicians, and statesmen. They consume while producing nothing. Although no physiocrat himself, Adam Smith was influenced by them and felt compelled on these grounds to acknowledge the superior productivity of agriculture over all other pursuits.

Particular physiocratic doctrines help explain other aspects of Jefferson's policies, too. Anticipating the "iron law of wages," physiocrats taught that competition always drives wages down to subsistence levels. Therefore, Jefferson had special reason to fear the wretchedness caused by industrial employment and to prize the independence of the self-employed landowner. Government debt, physiocrats believed, was a curse upon any society, since it had no other effect than to transfer to the unproductive classes wealth which might otherwise be used to improve agriculture. Finally, according to the physiocrats, government restrictions on trade, such as tariffs, normally work to depress farm prices relative to the cost of other goods, whereas above all else national prosperity demands a "good price" (*bon prix*) for agriculture.

In fact, underlying all this theory was the indisputable reality of the *bon prix* enjoyed by agriculture during Jefferson's lifetime. After the middle of the eighteenth century Europe was no longer able to produce all the foodstuffs required by its growing urban population. As a result, as much of North America as could be put to the plow was turned into an enormous breadbasket for the Atlantic world. The thin soil of New England and the hot climate of the lower South were unsuitable for grain crops, but most American farmers lived between these extremes. From New York to Georgia and as far west as settlements and transportation could be pushed, they were raising wheat. Even the tobacco planters of the Chesapeake region converted to grain during these years. As Thomas Paine had remarked, "so long as eating is the custom of Europe,"

Americans, it appeared, could count on unrivalled prosperity by following the plow.

Thomas Jefferson's manuscripts fill many volumes, but in his lifetime he published only a single, slender book. The following selections illustrate his lifelong preoccupations.

Query VI

❀ There is an infinitude of . . . plants and flowers, for an enumeration and scientific description of which I must refer to the *Flora Virginica* of our great botanist, Dr. Clayton,[1] published by Gronovius at Leyden, in 1762. This accurate observer was a native and resident of this state, passed a long life in exploring and describing its plants, and is supposed to have enlarged the botanical catalogue as much as almost any man who has lived.

Besides these plants, which are native, our *farms* produce wheat, rye, barley, oats, buck-wheat, broom corn,[2] and Indian corn. The climate suits rice well enough, wherever the lands do. Tobacco, hemp, flax, and cotton are staple commodities. Indigo yields two cuttings. The silk-worm is a native, and the mulberry, proper for its food, grows kindly.

We cultivate, also, potatoes, both the long and the round, turnips, carrots, parsnips, pumpkins, and ground nuts (*arachis*).[3] Our grasses are lucerne,[4] saintfoin, burnet, timothy, ray,[5] and orchard grass; red, white, and yellow clover; greensward, blue grass, and crab grass.

The *gardens* yield musk-melons, water-melons, tomatoes, okra, pomegranates, figs, and the esculent plants of Europe.

The *orchards* produce apples, pears, cherries, quinces, peaches, nectarines, apricots, almonds, and plums. . . .

---

[1] John Clayton (1686–1773), botanist and Clerk of Gloucester County. Jefferson erred in supposing him to be a native of Virginia; he was born in England.

[2] Stiff grass used in making brooms and brushes.

[3] Peanuts.

[4] Alfalfa.

[5] Ryegrass.

Query VII

A more satisfactory estimate of our climate to some, may perhaps be formed by noting the plants which grow here, subject, however, to be killed by our severest colds. These are the fig, pomegranate, artichoke, and European walnut. In mild winters, lettuce and endive require no shelter; but, generally, they need a slight covering. . . .

A change in our climate, however, is taking place very sensibly.[6] Both heats and colds are become much more moderate within the memory even of the middle-aged. Snows are less frequent and less deep. They do not often lie, below the mountains, more than one, two, or three days, and very rarely a week. They are remembered to have been formerly frequent, deep, and of long continuance. The elderly inform me, the earth used to be covered with snow about three months in every year. The rivers, which then seldom failed to freeze over in the course of the winter, scarcely ever do so now. This change has produced an unfortunate fluctuation between heat and cold, in the spring of the year, which is very fatal to fruits. From the year 1741 to 1769, an interval of twenty-eight years, there was no instance of fruit killed by the frost in the neighborhood of Monticello. An intense cold, produced by constant snows, kept the buds locked up till the sun could obtain, in the spring of the year, so fixed an ascendency as to dissolve those snows, and protect the buds, during their development, from every danger of returning cold. The accumulated snows of the winter remaining to be dissolved all together in the spring, produced those overflowings of our rivers, so frequent then, and so rare now. . . .

Query XIX

We never had an interior trade of any importance. Our exterior commerce has suffered very much from the beginning of the present contest.[7] During this time we have manufactured within our families the most necessary articles of clothing. Those of cotton will

---

[6]Perhaps Jefferson here notes the warming of the Northern Hemisphere in the wake of the "little ice age" of the seventeenth century.

[7]The Revolutionary War.

bear some comparison with the same kinds of manufacture in Europe; but those of wool, flax and hemp are very coarse, unsightly, and unpleasant; and such is our attachment to agriculture, and such our preference for foreign manufactures, that be it wise or unwise, our people will certainly return as soon as they can, to the raising raw materials, and exchanging them for finer manufactures than they are able to execute themselves.

The political economists of Europe have established it as a principle, that every State should endeavor to manufacture for itself; and this principle, like many others, we transfer to America, without calculating the difference of circumstance which should often produce a difference of result. In Europe the lands are either cultivated, or locked up against the cultivator. Manufacture must therefore be resorted to of necessity not of choice, to support the surplus of their people. But we have an immensity of land courting the industry of the husbandman. Is it best then that all our citizens should be employed in its improvement, or that one half should be called off from that to exercise manufactures and handicraft arts for the other? Those who labour in the earth are the chosen people of God, if ever he had a chosen people, whose breasts he has made his peculiar deposit for substantial and genuine virtue. It is the focus in which he keeps alive that sacred fire, which otherwise might escape from the face of the earth. Corruption of morals in the mass of cultivators is a phenomenon of which no age nor nation has furnished an example. It is the mark set on those, who, not looking up to heaven, to their own soil and industry, as does the husbandman, for their subsistence, depend for it on casualties and caprice of customers. Dependence begets subservience and venality, suffocates the germ of virtue, and prepares fit tools for the designs of ambition. This, the natural progress and consequence of the arts, has sometimes perhaps been retarded by accidental circumstances; but, generally speaking, the proportion which the aggregate of the other classes of citizens bears in any State to that of its husbandmen, is the proportion of its unsound to its healthy parts, and is a good enough barometer whereby to measure its degree of corruption. While we have land to labour then, let us never wish to see our citizens occupied at a workbench, or twirling a distaff.[8] Carpenters, masons, smiths, are wanting in husbandry; but, for the general operations of manufacture, let our workshops remain in Europe. It

---

[8]Traditional implement used in spinning.

is better to carry provisions and materials to workmen there, than bring them to the provisions and materials, and with them their manners and principles. The loss by the transportation of commodities across the Atlantic will be made up in happiness and permanence of government. The mobs of great cities add just so much to the support of pure government, as sores do to the strength of the human body. It is the manners and spirit of a people which preserve a republic in vigor. A degeneracy in these is a canker which soon eats to the heart of its laws and constitution. . . .

Query XX

In the year 1758 we exported seventy thousand hogsheads of tobacco, which was the greatest quantity ever produced in this country in one year. But its culture was fast declining at the commencement of this war and that of wheat taken its place; and it must continue to decline on the return of peace. I suspect that the change in the temperature of our climate has become sensible to that plant, which to be good, requires an extraordinary degree of heat. But it requires still more indispensably an uncommon fertility of soil; and the price which it commands at market will not enable the planter to produce this by manure. Was the supply still to depend on Virginia and Maryland alone as its culture becomes more difficult, the price would rise so as to enable the planter to surmount those difficulties and to live. But the western country on the Mississippi, and the midlands of Georgia, having fresh and fertile lands in abundance, and a hotter sun, will be able to undersell these two States, and will oblige them to abandon the raising of tobacco altogether. And a happy obligation for them it will be. It is a culture productive of infinite wretchedness. Those employed in it are in a continual state of exertion beyond the power of nature to support. Little food of any kind is raised by them; so that the men and animals on these farms are badly fed, and the earth is rapidly impoverished. The cultivation of wheat is the reverse in every circumstance. Besides clothing the earth with herbage, and preserving its fertility, it feeds the laborers plentifully, requires from them only a moderate toil, except in the season of harvest, raises great numbers of animals for food and service, and diffuses plenty and happiness among the whole. We find it easier to make an hundred bushels of wheat than a thousand weight of tobacco, and they are worth more when made. The weavil indeed is a formidable obstacle to the cultivation of this grain with us. But principles are already known which must lead to a remedy.

❖ ❖ ❖

No one ever did more than Jefferson to encourage the expansion of American agriculture. Wherever he travelled he noted unfamiliar plants and new farm implements, turning his home farm Monticello into an early agricultural experiment station. In public life the questions which most deeply engaged him were those which concerned putting as much of the continent as possible under cultivation and marketing the bountiful harvest of American farms. He was an early advocate of the cheap disposal of government land in the West directly to farmers. The extinction of Indian land title and the removal of the natives from the path of settlement were projects he energetically favored. As president, he seized the opportunity to purchase Louisiana, doubling the size of the United States in one stroke and winning control of the great river which gave western farmers access to the markets of the world. In retirement he meditated on the possibility of a war with Spain, which would permit the United States to capture Mexico and bring Cuba into the union as a new state. He dreamed of wresting Canada from the British. Then, he wrote to President Madison, "we should have such an empire for liberty as she has never surveyed since creation."

2

Alexander Hamilton
❖ ❖ ❖

Report on Manufactures
1791

*D*espite the priority accorded to birth and fortune in the pre-industrial world, there was more social mobility than is often supposed. Much of it was "sponsored," as the already-powerful recruited useful talent, sometimes advancing the quite humbly born to positions of great eminence.

Alexander Hamilton was one such example. Although he was a penniless youth from the West Indies, he was also handsome, charming, high-spirited, and preternaturally bright. In New York his exceptional talents were quickly recognized and encouraged. During the Revolution Washington attached the young man to his personal staff. Afterwards Hamilton contracted a superbly advantageous marriage to the daughter of Philip Schuyler, the great New York merchant, whose family had run Albany as a satrapy since the seventeenth century. Schuyler was as proud of his brilliant son-in-law as his daughter was enamored of him, and under his patronage Hamilton's political career flourished. At Schuyler's behest New York sent him to the Constitutional Convention, in which he took a celebrated part. When Washington became president, he appointed his former subaltern to head the largest department in the new government, the Treasury.

In Britain the First Lord of the Treasury is by definition Prime Minister, and it was a role from which the Anglophile Hamilton did not shrink. With his customary audacity he laid before Congress a series of

REPORT ON MANUFACTURES   From "Manufactures: Communicated to the House of Representatives, December 5, 1791," *American State Papers* (Washington, D.C.: Gales and Seaton, 1832–61), V, 123–27.

four reports which proposed to provide the United States with all the sophisticated financial apparatus, including a funded debt and a national bank, which earlier in the century had laid the foundation for Britain's commercial supremacy.

In the *Report on Manufactures*, Hamilton proposed to follow the British example in yet another way and industrialize the United States. He recommended a system of protective tariffs and prohibitions on imported goods to shield infant American industries from overseas competition. Had Hamilton had his way, the Industrial Revolution would have begun in the United States in the 1790s instead of at least a generation later.

Much of the *Report on Manufactures* was devoted to a refutation of the common opinion, set forth by the physiocrats and endorsed by Adam Smith, that manufacturing was inherently less productive than agriculture. To this end Hamilton cleverly turned Smith's argument upon itself. In one of his most famous passages Smith had identified the division of labor as the great secret of increased productivity. Hamilton supposed that manufacturing was capable of a greater division of labor than agriculture and hence was at least potentially the more productive. Of course he was right. It is estimated that during the first half of the nineteenth century in the United States the yearly output of a worker in a non-agricultural occupation was almost double that of a farm laborer.

❖ The expediency of encouraging manufactures in the United States, which was not long since deemed very questionable, appears at this time to be pretty generally admitted. The embarrassments which have obstructed the progress of our external trade have led to serious reflections on the necessity of enlarging the sphere of our domestic commerce. The restrictive regulations, which in foreign markets abridge the vent of the increasing surplus of our agricultural produce,[1] serve to beget an earnest desire that a more extensive demand for that surplus may be created at home. And the complete success which has rewarded manufacturing enterprise, in some valuable branches, . . . justif[ies] a hope that the

---

[1]Deprived of their normal markets within the British Empire, American agricultural exports had collapsed after 1772. During the 1780s Britain excluded the United States from the important West Indian trade, and when Hamilton wrote in 1791, even the limited trade concessions won by Jay's Treaty of 1794 had not yet been negotiated. Per capita American exports were still much less than they had been before the Revolution.

obstacles to the growth of this species of industry are less formidable than they were apprehended to be, and that it is not difficult to find in its further extension . . . an accession of resources favorable to national independence and safety.

There still are, nevertheless, respectable patrons of opinions unfriendly to the encouragement of manufactures. The following are, substantially, the arguments by which these opinions are defended.

In every country (say those who entertain them) agriculture is the most beneficial and *productive* object of human industry. This position, generally if not universally true, applies with peculiar emphasis to the United States, on account of their immense tracts of fertile territory, uninhabited and unimproved. Nothing can afford so advantageous an employment for capital and labor, as the conversion of this extensive wilderness into cultivated farms. Nothing equally with this, can contribute to the population, strength and real riches of the country. . . .

It ought readily to be conceded that the cultivation of the earth, as the primary and most certain source of national supply; as the immediate and chief source of subsistence to man; as the principle source of those materials which constitute the nutriment of other kinds of labor; as including a state most favorable to the freedom and independence of the human mind—one, perhaps, most conducive to the multiplication of the human species; has instrinsically a strong claim to pre-eminence over every other kind of industry.

But that it has a title to anything like an exclusive predilection, in any country, ought to be admitted with great caution. That it is even more productive than every other branch of industry requires more evidence than has yet been given. . . . That its real interests, precious and important as . . . they truly are, will be advanced, rather than injured by the due encouragement of manufactures, may, it is believed, be satisfactorily demonstrated. . . .

It has been maintained that agriculture is not only the most productive, but the only productive species of industry. . . . To this it has been answered[2] . . . that manufacturing labor reproduces a value equal to that which is expended or consumed in carrying it on, and continues in existence the original stock or capital employed. . . . If the consumption for any given period amounted to a

---

[2]Here Hamilton paraphrases Adam Smith's central argument against the supposed "sterility" of manufactures.

given sum, and the *increased* value of the produce manufactured in the same period to a *like sum*, the total amount of the consumption and production during that period would be equal to the *two sums*. . . . Though the increment of value produced by the classes of artificers should at no time exceed the value of the produce of the land consumed by them, yet there would be at every moment, in consequence of their labor, a greater value of goods in the market than would exist independent of it. . . .

But while the *exclusive* productiveness of agricultural labor has been thus denied and refuted, the superiority of its productiveness has been conceded without hesitation. . . .

It is extremely probable, that, on a full and accurate development of the matter, . . . it would be discovered that there is no material difference between the aggregate productiveness of the one, and of the other kind of industry. . . . Without contending for the superior productiveness of manufacturing industry, it may conduce to a better judgment of the policy which ought to be pursued respecting its encouragement, to contemplate the subject under some additional aspects, tending not only to confirm the idea that this kind of industry has been improperly represented as unproductive in itself, but to evince in addition that the establishment and diffusion of manufactures have the effect of rendering the total mass of useful and productive labor in a community *greater than it would otherwise be*. . . .

It has justly been observed that there is scarcely anything of greater moment in the economy of a nation than the proper division of labor. The separation of occupations causes each to be carried to a much greater perfection than it could possibly acquire if they were blended. This arises principally from three circumstances. 1st. The greater skill and dexterity naturally resulting from a constant and undivided application to a single object. . . . 2nd. The economy of time, by avoiding the loss of it incident to a frequent transition from one operation to another of a different nature. . . . 3rd. An extension of the use of machinery. A man occupied on a single object will have it more in his power . . . to exert his imagination in devising methods to facilitate and abridge labor, than if he were perplexed by a variety of . . . dissimilar operations. . . .

The employment of machinery forms an item of great importance in the general mass of national industry. 'Tis an artificial force brought in aid of the natural force of man; and to all the purposes of labor is an increase of hands, an accession of strength, unencumbered too by the expense of maintaining the laborer. May it not, therefore, be fairly inferred that those occupations which give greatest scope to the use of this auxiliary, contribute most to the general stock of industrious effort and, in consequence, to the general product of industry?

It shall be taken for granted . . . that manufacturing pursuits are susceptible in a greater degree of the application of machinery than those of agriculture. If so, all the difference is lost to a community which, instead of manufacturing for itself, procures the fabrics requisite to its supply from other countries. The substitution of foreign for domestic manufactures is a transfer to foreign nations of the advantages accruing from the employment of machinery, in the modes in which it is capable of being employed with most utility and to the greatest extent.

The cotton mill, invented in England within the last twenty years,[3] is a signal illustration of the general proposition which has been just advanced. In consequence of it, all the different processes for spinning cotton are performed by means of machines, which are put in motion by water, and attended chiefly by women and children, and by a smaller number of persons, in the whole, than are requisite in the ordinary mode of spinning. And it is an advantage of great moment that the operations of this mill continue with convenience during the night as well as through the day. The prodigious effect of such a machine is easily conceived. . . .

In places where those institutions prevail, besides the persons regularly engaged in them, they afford occasional and extra employment to industrious individuals and families who are willing to devote the leisure resulting from the intermissions of their ordinary pursuits to collateral labors, as a resource for multiplying their acquisitions or their enjoyments. The husbandman himself experiences a new source of profit and support from the increased industry of his wife and daughters, invited and stimulated by the demands of the neighboring manufactories.

Besides this advantage of occasional employment to classes having different occupations, there is another . . . of a similar tendency. This is the employment of persons who would otherwise be idle, and in many cases a burthen on the community, either from the bias of temper, habit, infirmity of body, or some other cause . . . disqualifying them for the toils of the country. It is worthy of particular remark that, in general, women and children are rendered

---

[3]Sir Richard Arkwright patented his spinning frame in 1769.

more useful, and the latter more early useful, by manufacturing establishments, than they would otherwise be.[4] Of the number of persons employed in the cotton manufactories of Great Britain, it is computed that four-sevenths, nearly, are women and children; of whom the greatest proportion are children, and many of them of a tender age.

And thus it appears to be one of the attributes of manufactures, and one of no small consequence, to give occasion to the exertion of a greater quantity of industry, even by the *same number* of persons, where they happen to prevail, than would exist if there were no such establishments. . . .

It is a just observation that minds of the strongest and most active powers for their proper objects fall below mediocrity and labor without effect if confined to uncongenial pursuits. And it is thence to be inferred that the results of human exertion may be immensely increased by diversifying its objects. When all the different kinds of industry obtain in a community, each individual can find his proper element, and can call into activity the whole vigour of his nature. And the community is benefitted by the services of its respective members in the manner in which each can serve it with most effect.

If there be anything in a remark often to be met with, namely, that there is in the genius of the people of this country a peculiar aptitude for mechanic improvements, it would operate as a forcible reason for giving opportunities to the exercise of that species of talent by the propagation of manufactures. . . .

To cherish and stimulate the activity of the human mind, by multiplying the objects of enterprise, is not among the least considerable of the expedients by which the wealth of a nation may be promoted. Even things in themselves not positively advantageous, sometimes become so by their tendency to provoke exertion. Every new scene which is opened to the busy nature of man to rouse and exert itself, is the addition of a new energy to the general stock of effort.

The spirit of enterprise, useful and prolific as it is, must necessarily be contracted or expanded in proportion to the simplicity or variety of the occupations and productions which are to be found in a society. It must be less in a nation of mere cultivators, than in

---

[4]It should be remembered that women and children had always been allotted the tedious chore of spinning by hand, and that rural children were always put to work as soon as they were able, often at heavier tasks than those Hamilton proposed.

a nation of cultivators and merchants; less in a nation of cultivators and merchants, than in a nation of cultivators, artificers, and merchants.

⊞ ⊞ ⊞

The *Report on Manufactures* was the only one of Hamilton's reports which Congress declined to enact. It adopted some of the recommended tariffs, but until 1816 the purpose was revenue, not protection. In 1793 war broke out between Britain and France, and during the following two decades of world conflict American businessmen could earn far greater profits in foreign trade than they could hope to realize in manufacturing. Not until overseas commerce was interrupted by the Embargo of 1807 and the War of 1812 did manufacturing get under way in the United States. Even then, with the exception of protective tariffs, the kinds of government assistance Hamilton had recommended were more forthcoming from the states than from the federal goverment.

Hamilton had urged Congress to establish a national board with ample funds to subsidize industrial pilot projects. When Congress failed to act, Hamilton lent his patronage as Secretary of the Treasury and his personal supervision to a private Society for Establishing Useful Manufactures, which was incorporated in 1791 in New Jersey—the first New Jersey business corporation. The Society was authorized to raise $1 million in capital, largely in the funded debt of the United States. It hired Major Pierre L'Enfant, who had just planned the new federal capital on the Potomac, to lay out a grand "federal manufacturing city" on a site at the falls of the Passaic River to be named Paterson. Canals were dug to power the cotton mill erected there, and English mechanics were hired by the Society to try to duplicate some of the new British textile machinery. During the nineteenth century Paterson, New Jersey, became one of the premier industrial cities of the nation. By 1814 there were eleven cotton mills and several other kinds of factories in operation. By mid century silk weaving had surpassed cotton in importance, and at its peak in 1912 Paterson accounted for almost half the nation's production of silk cloth. Before 1900 most of the nation's steam locomotives were built in Paterson works. The Colt revolver was also first manufactured there; its inventor Samuel Colt was nephew to the first mill superintendent hired by Hamilton's Society for Useful Manufactures. The Society itself remained in business until 1946.

3

Thomas Jefferson
❀ ❀ ❀

First Inaugural Address
1801

Before 1789, Thomas Jefferson and Alexander Hamilton had little contact with one another. While Jefferson was shining at the Second Continental Congress, Hamilton was an obscure New Yorker, only twenty-one years of age. During the Revolutionary War, Hamilton was making his mark as George Washington's *aide de camp*, while Jefferson was governor of Virginia and, by choice, uninvolved in the military. When the Constitution was being written and ratified, Jefferson was abroad, American Minister to France.

Brought together for the first time in Washington's cabinet— Jefferson as Secretary of State, Hamilton as Secretary of the Treasury— the two men discovered they did not like each other. Incompatible personalities and rival ambitions were part of the conflict. Neither man was the sort to play second fiddle to anyone except George Washington. Both men were determined to shape the new Republic (and Washington) according to their own principles. But they differed on fundamental points.

Jefferson was content that agriculture should remain the economic foundation of the United States, and he considered the sole function of

FIRST INAUGURAL ADDRESS   From *The Writings of Thomas Jefferson*, ed. H. A. Washington (Washington: Taylor and Maury, 1854), VIII, 1–6.

republican government to be the suppression of disorder and defense of citizens' liberties. Hamilton's vision of a bustling commercial and industrial nation, on the other hand, required the national government to take strong initiative in encouraging financial and industrial entrepreneurs by adopting policies that favored them.

It was Hamilton who had his way with Washington and, for the most part, with Congress. The president respectfully heard Jefferson's arguments against funding the national debt, assuming the debts of the states, and establishing the first Bank of the United States, actions which would enhance the power of the federal government. Then Washington, and a majority of Congress, rejected them.

In 1793, a frustrated Jefferson resigned from the cabinet and quietly encouraged criticism of the administration. The political parties, Federalists and Republicans, which all had once hoped would not develop became a reality.

During Washington's second term and the succeeding presidency of John Adams, party lines grew clearer and party hatreds deeper. When Jefferson declared in the Kentucky Resolutions (1798–99) that the individual states had the right to declare a law of Congress unconstitutional, and therefore null and void within its boundaries, Federalists believed he was trying to destroy the federal union, the only thing that stood between the United States and anarchy!

Much more troubling to Federalists, particularly in New England, was Jefferson's support of revolutionary France, a nation which had executed thousands and plunged Europe into a series of vicious wars. When Jefferson stood for president against John Adams in 1800, New England pulpits trembled as preachers warned that his election would mean France in North America, "dwellings in flames, hoary hairs bathed in blood, female chastity violated, children writhing on the pike."

The Republicans won the election, but because of a quirk in the Constitution (later amended) Jefferson won no more votes in the electoral college than his vice-presidential running mate, Aaron Burr. Seizing this opportunity to thwart Jefferson's victory, many Federalists threw their support to Burr. They hoped that if they gave him the prize of the presidency, the opportunistic New Yorker would align himself with their party.

However, Mad Tom's old enemy, Alexander Hamilton, disagreed. Much as he disliked Jefferson, he did not care to see the government he had done so much to create disintegrate because of a constitutional quirk. Moreover, while he regarded Jefferson as fatuous, he despised Burr as ill-intentioned. His influence in the Federalist party helped carry the day. Jefferson was finally elected shortly before Inauguration Day.

Jefferson also was determined that the federal union should not fall. After taking the oath of office, he delivered an address that seemed to set partisanship aside. Clearly, the new president wanted to console fearful Federalists and, as usual, he was extremely eloquent.

❄ *Friends and Fellow-Citizens:*

Called upon to undertake the duties of the first executive office of our country, I avail myself of the presence of that portion of my fellow citizens which is here assembled to express my grateful thanks for the favor with which they have been pleased to look toward me, to declare a sincere consciousness that the task is above my talents, and that I approach it with those anxious and awful presentiments which the greatness of the charge and the weakness of my powers so justly inspire. A rising nation, spread over a wide and fruitful land, traversing all the seas with the rich productions of their industry, engaged in commerce with nations who feel power and forget right, advancing rapidly to destinies beyond the reach of mortal eye—when I contemplate these transcendent objects, and see the honor, the happiness, and the hopes of this beloved country committed to the issue and the auspices of this day, I shrink from the contemplation, and humble myself before the magnitude of the undertaking. Utterly indeed should I despair did not the presence of many whom I here see remind me that in the other high authorities provided by our Constitution I shall find resources of wisdom, of virtue, and of zeal on which to rely under all difficulties. To you then, gentlemen, who are charged with the sovereign functions of legislation, and to those associated with you, I look with encouragement for that guidance and support which may enable us to steer with safety the vessel in which we are all embarked amidst the conflicting elements of a troubled world.

During the contest of opinion through which we have passed, the animation of discussions and of exertions has sometimes worn an aspect which might impose on[1] strangers unused to think freely and to speak and to write what they think. But being now decided by the voice of the nation, enounced[2] according to the rules of the constitution, all will of course arrange themselves under the will of the law, and unite in common efforts for the common good. All too will bear in mind this sacred principle, that though the will of the majority is in all cases to prevail, that will, to be rightful, must be reasonable; that the minority possess their equal rights, which equal laws must protect, and to violate would be oppression. Let us then, fellow citizens, unite with one heart and one mind, let us restore to social intercourse that harmony and affection without which liberty and even life itself are but dreary things. And let us reflect that,

---

[1]Mislead.
[2]Enunciated.

having banished from our land that religious intolerance under which mankind so long bled and suffered, we have yet gained little if we countenance a political intolerance as despotic, as wicked, and capable of as bitter and bloody persecutions. During the throes and convulsions of the ancient world, during the agonizing spasms of infuriated man, seeking through blood and slaughter his long lost liberty, it was not wonderful that the agitation of the billows should reach even this distant and peaceful shore; that this should be more felt and feared by some and less by others, and should divide opinions as to measures of safety; but every difference of opinion is not a difference of principle. We have called by different names brethren of the same principle. We are all republicans: we are all federalists.[3] If there be any among us who wish to dissolve this Union or to change its republican form, let them stand undisturbed, as monuments of the safety with which error of opinion may be tolerated where reason is left free to combat it. I know, indeed, that some honest men fear that a republican government cannot be strong, that this government is not strong enough. But would the honest patriot, in the full tide of successful experiment, abandon a government which has so far kept us free and firm on the theoretic and visionary fear that this government, the world's best hope, may, by possibility, want energy to preserve itself? I trust not. I believe this, on the contrary, the strongest government on earth. I believe it the only one where every man, at the call of the law, would fly to the standard of the law, and would meet invasions of the public order as his own personal concern. Sometimes it is said that man cannot be trusted with the government of himself. Can he, then, be trusted with the government of others? Or have we found angels in the form of kings to govern him? Let history answer this question.

Let us then pursue with courage and confidence our own federal and republican principles, our attachment to union and representative government. Kindly separated by nature, and a wide ocean, from the exterminating havoc of one quarter of the globe; too high-minded to endure the degradations of the others; possessing a chosen country, with room enough for our descendants to the thousandth and thousandth generation; entertaining a due sense of our equal right to the use of our own faculties, to the acquisitions of our own industry, to honor and confidence from our fellow citi-

---

[3]Notice that Jefferson uses lowercase letters. Sometimes, and quite incorrectly, this famous sentence is written "We are all Republicans; we are all Federalists," as if Jefferson were repudiating the very existence of the political parties. In truth, he wished only to emphasize the similarity of both parties' basic principles.

zens, resulting not from birth, but from our actions and their sense of them; enlightened by a benign religion, professed, indeed, and practiced in various forms, yet all of them inculcating honesty, truth, temperance, gratitude, and the love of man; acknowledging and adoring an overruling providence, which by all its dispensations proves that it delights in the happiness of man here and his greater happiness hereafter—with all these blessings, what more is necessary to make us a happy and a prosperous people? Still one thing more, fellow citizens—a wise and frugal government, which shall restrain men from injuring one another, shall leave them otherwise free to regulate their own pursuits of industry and improvement, and shall not take from the mouth of labor the bread it has earned. This is the sum of good government, and this is necessary to close the circle of our felicities.

❀ ❀ ❀

Warm sentiments are not cold policies. Jefferson's address did not foretell the character of his administration. Far from being a president of compromise and conciliation, he was more deliberately partisan than either of his predecessors had been. He denied an apparently legitimate government appointment to Federalist William Marbury. He supported the impeachment of one Federalist Supreme Court Justice and hoped to remove Chief Justice John Marshall from office. And he pursued a foreign policy that was disastrous for the commerce of Federalist New England.

More significant, however, was President Jefferson's quiet abandonment of policies he had voiced when in the opposition in favor of alternatives that could only be called federalistic. Nothing more was heard of the states' right of nullification. Despite the power to do so, Jefferson did not molest the Federalists' Bank of the United States. However, these actions (or lack of action) were not carried out in the spirit of the statement "We are all federalists. We are all republicans." On the contrary, the aggressive partisanship of Jefferson's Republicans was to succeed, by 1817, in virtually extirpating the party of Washington, Hamilton, and Adams.

4

Thomas Jefferson

❋ ❋ ❋

Letters to R. R. Livingston and John Breckinridge

1802, 1803

*I*n none of his presidential actions did
Thomas Jefferson depart more radically from his pre-presidential
philosophy of government than in his 1803 authorization of the purchase
of Louisiana from France. In the debates with Hamilton in Washington's
cabinet, Jefferson had argued that the federal government was enjoined
from exercising any power not specifically allotted it in the Constitution. It
was on the grounds that the Constitution did not specifically give Congress
the right to charter a national bank, for instance, that Jefferson opposed
Hamilton's Bank of the United States. His viewpoint is usually
characterized as "strict construction" of the Constitution. Hamilton's
"broad construction" of the Constitution, by contrast, held that the federal
government was entitled to exercise any power not specifically denied it in
the document.

The Constitution empowered the president to negotiate treaties
"with the advice and consent of the Senate." However, the Constitution had
no specific provision empowering either the president or Congress to
acquire additional territory for the republic. Therefore, from a strict-

LETTERS TO R. R. LIVINGSTON AND JOHN BRECKINRIDGE   From *The Writings of Thomas
Jefferson*, ed. H. A. Washington (Washington: Taylor and Maury, 1854), IV, 431–34,
498–501.

constructionist point of view, it was highly dubious when, in 1802, Jefferson instructed Robert R. Livingston, the American Minister in Paris, to offer France $2 million for a tract of land on the lower Mississippi River to be used as an American port.

Because the Constitution unambivalently states that Congress alone has the power to appropriate funds for any purpose, Jefferson behaved even more dubiously when, in January, 1803, he dispatched James Monroe to join Livingston in Paris with instructions to offer the $2 million for the purchase of New Orleans and West Florida (coastal Alabama and Mississippi). Failing to strike that bargain, Monroe was to raise the ante as high as $10 million, a figure that had never appeared in any Congressional allocation or presidential communication to Congress!

Having so finely spun the concept of strict construction, why would a man issue secret orders which mocked it so extraordinarily? The answer is to be found in two of Jefferson's letters: one to Livingston in April, 1802, shortly after France had taken control of Louisiana, and the other to Senator John Breckinridge of Kentucky in August, 1803, after Livingston and Monroe had swung a deal beyond Jefferson's imaginings.

To Robert R. Livingston
April 18, 1802

❀ The cession of Louisiana and the Floridas[1] by Spain to France, works most sorely on the United States. On this subject the Secretary of State has written to you fully, yet I cannot forbear recurring to it personally, so deep is the impression it makes on my mind. It completely reverses all the political relations of the United States, and will form a new epoch in our political course. Of all nations of any consideration, France is the one which, hitherto, has offered the fewest points on which we could have any conflict of right, and the most points of a communion of interests. From these causes, we have ever looked to her as our *natural friend*, as one with which we never could have an occasion of difference. . . .

---

[1] Americans then thought of Florida as two provinces. The present state of Florida was East Florida. The gulf coast of Alabama and Mississippi, including the ports of Mobile and Biloxi, were West Florida.

[However,] there is on the globe one single spot, the possessor of which is our natural and habitual enemy. It is New Orleans, through which the produce of three-eighths of our territory must pass to market, and from its fertility it will ere long yield more than half of our whole produce, and contain more than half of our inhabitants. France, placing herself in that door, assumes to us the attitude of defiance. . . . These circumstances render it impossible that France and the United States can continue long friends, when they meet in so irritable a position. They, as well as we, must be blind if they do not see this; and we must be very improvident if we do not begin to make arrangements on that hypothesis. The day that France takes possession of New Orleans, fixes the sentence which is to restrain her forever within her low-water mark. It seals the union of two nations, who, in conjunction, can maintain exclusive possession of the ocean. From that moment, we must marry ourselves to the British fleet and nation. We must turn all our attention to a maritime force, for which our resources place us on very high ground; and having formed and connected together a power which may render reinforcement of her settlements here impossible to France, make the first cannon which shall be fired in Europe the signal for the tearing up [of] any settlement she may have made. . . .

If France considers Louisiana, however, as indispensable for her views, she might perhaps be willing to look about for arrangements which might reconcile it to our interests. If anything could do this, it would be the ceding to us the island of New Orleans and the Floridas. This would certainly, in a great degree, remove the causes of jarring and irritation between us, and perhaps for such a length of time, as might produce other means of making the measure permanently conciliatory to our interests and friendships. It would, at any rate, relieve us from the necessity of taking immediate measures for countervailing such an operation by arrangements in another quarter. But still we should consider New Orleans and the Floridas as no equivalent for the risk of a quarrel with France, produced by her vicinage.[2] . . .

Every eye in the United States is now fixed on the affairs of Louisiana. Perhaps nothing since the revolutionary war, has produced more uneasy sensations through the body of the nation. Notwithstanding temporary bickerings have taken place with France, she has still a strong hold on the affections of our citizens generally. I have thought it not amiss, by way of supplement to the letters of

---

[2]Nearness or proximity.

the Secretary of State, to write you this private one, to impress you with the importance we affix to this transaction. . . .

To John Breckinridge
August 12, 1803

Our information as to the country is very incomplete; we have taken measures to obtain it full as to the settled part, which I hope to receive in time for Congress. . . . In the meanwhile, without waiting for permission, we shall enter into the exercise of the natural right we have always insisted on with Spain, to wit, that of a nation holding the upper part of streams, having a right of innocent passage through them to the ocean. We shall prepare her to see us practise on this, and she will not oppose it by force.[3]

Objections are raising to the eastward against the vast extent of our boundaries, and propositions are made to exchange Louisiana, or a part of it, for the Floridas. But, as I have said, we shall get the Floridas without, and I would not give one inch of the waters of the Mississippi to any nation, because I see in a light very important to our peace the exclusive right to its navigation, and the admission of no nation into it, but as into the Potomac or Delaware, with our consent and under our police. The future inhabitants of the Atlantic and Mississippi States will be our sons. We leave them in distinct but bordering establishments. We think we see their happiness in their union, and we wish it. Events may prove it otherwise; and if they see their interest in separation, why should we take side with our Atlantic rather than our Mississippi descendants? It is the elder and the younger son differing. God bless them both, and keep them in union, if it be for their good, but separate them, if it be better. The inhabited part of Louisiana, from Point Coupée to the sea, will of course be immediately a territorial government, and soon a State. But above that, the best use we can make of the country for some time, will be to give establishments in it to the Indians on the east side of the Mississippi, in exchange for their present country, and open land offices in the last, and thus make this acquisition the means of filling up the eastern side, instead of drawing off its pop-

---

[3]Jefferson refers to the "right of deposit"—the right of the Americans to use New Orleans as a port, which was agreed to by Spain in Pinckney's Treaty (1795), and cancelled by Napoleon when France announced its intention to take Louisiana from Spain.

ulation. When we shall be full on this side, we may lay off a range of States on the western bank from the head to the mouth, and so, range after range, advancing compactly as we multiply.

❈ ❈ ❈

Two days before James Monroe arrived in Paris, the French Foreign Minister, Charles Maurice de Talleyrand, summoned Robert Livingston and asked a question that flabbergasted him: How much would the United States pay for the whole of Louisiana? But it was not precisely clear to anyone just what the boundaries of such a purchase would be.

Until 1801, Louisiana had been Spanish, bordering on the older Spanish Viceroyalty of Mexico. Because the continent was so vast and the interior unpopulated by Europeans, no one had seen a need to explore the Rocky Mountains that marked the boundary between the two provinces. (Jefferson called them "high lands.") But it was clear that the Louisiana country measured something on the order of 820,000 square miles, making it almost as large as the United States of 1803.

The opportunity to purchase Louisiana was offered to the Americans because the sprawling province had ceased to be of any use to Napoleon. War with Great Britain was imminent, and even if Jefferson's prediction of an Anglo-American alliance was unknown to Napoleon, he was quite aware that the Royal Navy alone was up to conquering Louisiana.

Although Jefferson had only been interested in guaranteeing the right of Americans to trade freely on the Mississippi River, Livingston and Monroe jumped at Talleyrand's offer. Within two weeks they agreed on a purchase price of $15 million (about $19 per square mile).

Back in Washington, Jefferson found it easy to cope with his constitutional scruples. "A strict observance of the written laws," he wrote, "is doubtless one of the highest duties of a good citizen, but it is not the highest. To lose our country to a scrupulous adherence to written law would be . . . absurdly sacrificing the ends to the means." When New England Federalists persisted in reminding him of his former strict constructionist principles, he accused them of "metaphysical subtleties."

Elsewhere in his letter to Breckinridge, Jefferson made it clear that national interest took precedence over principle when an act of government "so much advances the good of the country." Acquiring Louisiana meant avoiding both war with France and diplomatic marriage to Great Britain. It meant a secure outlet for western crops, vast new opportunities in land for Americans, and a place west of the Mississippi to which the Indians might be pushed. Congress *did* ratify Jefferson's purchase and appropriate the money for it. As Talleyrand had said to Monroe and Livingston, "You have made a noble bargain for yourselves, and I suppose you will make the most of it."

5

James Monroe
❖ ❖ ❖

The Monroe Doctrine
1823

Jefferson's handpicked successor, James Madison, had an unhappy presidency. He was a brilliant political theorist, as the Federalist Papers and even the Virginia Resolutions clearly showed. But "Little Jemmy Applejohn" lacked the heroic associations with the Revolution that were attached to Jefferson. Short and frail, Madison cut an unimpressive physical presence in an age of men who, without dwelling on it, were inclined to be athletic. Most important, he presided over a war that amounted to a series of disasters and humiliations, until a single glorious American victory at New Orleans.

James Monroe, who succeeded Madison in 1817, lacked Madison's high order of intelligence. But Monroe is proof of the principle that good luck has as much to do with historical reputation as an individual's decisions and acts do.

Monroe was very lucky. He won his party's presidential nomination only because his rivals took no interest in the prize. He took office at a time when the old Federalist–Republican bitterness had been sweetened by patriotic pride in the young nation's numerous accomplishments. A Boston newspaper, and historians since, lauded his first term as "an era of good feelings." Finally, Monroe was fortunate in having as his Secretary of State John Quincy Adams, son of the second president and possessor of more true wisdom than the first five presidents combined.

THE MONROE DOCTRINE From *House Documents, Eighteenth Congress, First Session, 1823–24*, I (2), December 2, 1823, 13–15.

Quincy Adams had spent half his life abroad on a variety of diplomatic assignments, all dispatched with success. In 1819, as Monroe's Secretary of State, he made good on Jefferson's prediction about the future of Florida by cajoling Spain into ceding the peninsula to the United States. He was able to do this because the Spanish empire was falling apart. From Mexico to Tierra del Fuego, rebels had proclaimed and effectively established independent republics.

Spain's European allies had hinted they might contribute funds and troops to the cause of reasserting Spanish sovereignty in the Western Hemisphere. But Florida, lying vulnerable on the periphery of the old empire, was not particularly valuable to Spain. It seemed a small prize with which to appease the Americans.

Quincy Adams had no intention of being appeased, however. In privately discussing another matter of foreign policy in 1821, he said "We should assume distinctly the principle that the American continents are no longer subjects for any new colonial establishments." The British Foreign Minister provided a golden opportunity to declare this policy publicly when he quietly suggested that Great Britain and the United States jointly issue a proclamation to that effect.

Former presidents Jefferson and Madison urged James Monroe to accept the offer. They argued that, alone, the United States lacked the power to prevent any European military expedition in the Western Hemisphere but that Great Britain, with her worldwide navy, did.

Quincy Adams appreciated the point. Indeed, he surely knew that enforcement of his policy would rest largely with the Royal Navy. However, unlike the lifelong anglophobes Jefferson and Madison, he did not want the United States to "marry the British fleet" or, in his own words, become a "cockboat in the wake of the British man of war." He persuaded President Monroe to proclaim the end of the era of colonization in the Americas as a unilateral action of the United States.

Monroe spoke on a number of subjects in his address of December 2, 1823. But in order to emphasize his point, he returned with conspicuous repetitiveness to his twofold policy: the United States would not intervene in European affairs; European powers must not intervene in American affairs.

❀ The occasion has been judged proper for asserting, as a principle in which the rights and interests of the United States are involved, that the American continents, by the free and independent condition which they have assumed and maintain, are henceforth not to be considered as subjects for future colonization by any European powers. . . .

It was stated at the commencement of the last session, that a great effort was then making in Spain and Portugal, to improve the condition of the people of those countries; and that it appeared to be conducted with extraordinary moderation. It need scarcely be remarked, that the result has been, so far, very different from what was then anticipated. Of events in that quarter of the globe, with which we have so much intercourse, and from which we derive our origin, we have always been anxious and interested spectators. The citizens of the United States cherish sentiments the most friendly, in favor of the liberty and happiness of their fellow men on that side of the Atlantic. In the wars of the European powers, in matters relating to themselves, we have never taken any part, nor does it comport with our policy so to do. It is only when our rights are invaded, or seriously menaced, that we resent injuries, or make preparation for our defence. With the movements in this hemisphere, we are, of necessity, more immediately connected, and by causes which must be obvious to all enlightened and impartial observers. The political system of the allied powers is essentially different, in this respect, from that of America. This difference proceeds from that which exists in their respective governments. And to the defence of our own, which has been achieved by the loss of so much blood and treasure, and matured by the wisdom of their most enlightened citizens, and under which we have enjoyed unexampled felicity, this whole nation is devoted. We owe it, therefore, to candor, and to the amicable relations existing between the United States and those powers, to declare, that we should consider any attempt on their part to extend their system to any portion of this hemisphere, as dangerous to our peace and safety. With the existing colonies or dependencies of any European power, we have not interfered, and shall not interfere. But, with the governments who have declared their independence and maintained it, and whose independence we have, on great consideration, and on just principles, acknowledged, we could not view any interposition for the purpose of oppressing them, or controlling, in any other manner, their destiny, by any European power, in any other light than as the manifestation of an unfriendly disposition towards the United States. In the war between these new governments and Spain, we declared our neutrality at the time of their recognition, and to this we have adhered, and shall continue to adhere, provided no change shall occur, which, in the judgment of the competent authorities of this government, shall make a corresponding change, on the part of the United States, indispensable to their security. . . .

Our policy, in regard to Europe, which was adopted at an early stage of the wars which have so long agitated that quarter of the globe, nevertheless remains the same, which is, not to interfere in the internal concerns of any of its powers; to consider the government *de facto* as the legitimate government for us; to cultivate friendly relations with it, and to preserve those relations by a frank, firm, and manly policy, meeting, in all instances, the just claims of every power; submitting to injuries from none. But, in regard to [the American] continents, circumstances are eminently and conspicuously different. It is impossible that the allied powers should extend their political system to any portion of either continent, without endangering our peace and happiness; nor can any one believe that our Southern Brethren, if left to themselves, would adopt it of their own accord. It is equally impossible, therefore, that we should behold such interposition, in any form, with indifference. If we look to the comparative strength and resources of Spain and those new governments, and their distance from each other, it must be obvious that she can never subdue them. It is still the true policy of the United States, to leave the parties to themselves, in the hope that other powers will pursue the same course.

❊ ❊ ❊

Spain never did attempt to recolonize the Western Hemisphere. Thus, the "Monroe Doctrine," (as it later came to be known) was virtually forgotten until the supporters of James K. Polk, the Democratic party presidential candidate of 1844, quoted it as a warning to Great Britain over the possession of Oregon. That issue was settled by a favorable compromise, and as American interests in Latin America steadily increased, almost every president since has cited the Monroe Doctrine at one time or another, impressing it permanently in the national consciousness.

The most important invocation of the Monroe Doctrine was President Theodore Roosevelt's in 1902. Fearing that British and German naval forces were on the verge of occupying Venezuela in order to force cash reparations out of the Venezuelan government, Roosevelt proclaimed that whenever the "chronic wrong-doing" of a nation in the Western Hemisphere threatened to justify European intervention, the United States would intervene in order to preserve that nation's independence of Old World powers. This principle became known as the "Roosevelt Corollary" to the Monroe Doctrine.

It was a principle fraught with peril for the United States. Many nations of the Caribbean were poorly governed and chronically involved in financial difficulties with European and American bankers. Indeed, the U.S. government's promise of intervention in the affairs of other American nations encouraged private investment and loans. Financial interests and policy-makers alike came to look upon the Caribbean Sea as an American lake. At one time or another, United States Marines were sent into Cuba, Haiti, the Dominican Republic, and Nicaragua. In alliance with pliant and often corrupt local elites, American policy-makers virtually ran every Central American and Caribbean nation except Mexico.

So unpopular was this imperious "big brother" policy in Latin America that, during the 1930s, a series of American statesmen replaced it with the "Good Neighbor" Policy, which rejected the Roosevelt Corollary while clinging to the Monroe Doctrine. Not until the 1960s, when the regime of Fidel Castro in Cuba took a pro-Soviet turn, were American troops again used to occupy another American nation, the Dominican Republic.

In 1984 the return to interventionism was emphasized by the landing of American troops in the tiny island nation of Grenada. By that time, Latin American rebels claiming to represent the interests of the common people were more likely to look upon the United States, rather than any European nation, as the chief threat to their nations' hegemony and the Monroe Doctrine as the insidious ruse of *Yanqui imperialismo*.

PART 4

❖ ❖ ❖

Jacksonians and Whigs
1829–1848

1

Andrew Jackson

❖ ❖ ❖

Message on Removal of the Southern Indians

1829

*I*n addition to his renown as the
victor of New Orleans, Andrew Jackson was famed as an "Indian Fighter."
This was a proud title among westerners. Ever hungry for rich new lands,
they encroached constantly on the ranges of what Supreme Court Chief
Justice John Marshall called "a people, once numerous, powerful, and truly
independent, found by our ancestors in the quiet and uncontrolled
possession of an ample domain." Time and again, the native peoples were
reduced and despoiled, as they would be for a generation after Old
Hickory departed for his own happy hunting grounds.

By the time Jackson was elected president in 1828, the Indians of the
Old Northwest had long since been vanquished. These once numerous
tribes had simply disappeared, moved west of the Mississippi, or survived
as pathetic remnants on the fringes of white society.

In the Old Southwest, by contrast, the Chickasaw, Choctaw, Creek,
Seminole, and Cherokee nations had resisted white encroachment, partly
by battle, but principally by embracing the ways of life that made the
interlopers so powerful. The "Civilized Tribes" abandoned wandering and
hunting, a primitive economy requiring vast rangelands that were simply

MESSAGE ON REMOVAL OF THE SOUTHERN INDIANS   From *Message from the President of
the United States to the Two Houses of Congress at the Commencement of the First Session of
the Twenty-first Congress, December 8, 1829* (Washington: Duff Green, 1829).

not to be had in the agricultural republic. They settled down on large enclaves granted them by treaty with the federal government in Mississippi, Alabama, and Georgia. They lived in towns, elected leaders, and developed a written language which they taught in schools and in which they published newspapers. They raised the same cash crops grown by their white neighbors; cotton was king of the Civilized Tribes too. They even adopted the institution of Negro slavery that was the basis of staple production elsewhere in the South.

Because cotton cultivation was so lucrative, white southerners coveted the Indian lands for themselves. Their state governments, particularly Georgia's, harassed and pressured the Civilized Tribes throughout the 1820s. Georgia dangled incentives before the Cherokees in an effort to persuade them to move west and signed agreements with renegade chiefs. Georgia's congressmen lobbied Congress and President John Quincy Adams for a federal removal program. And in practice Georgia refused to acknowledge Cherokee sovereignty in any part of the state.

It was no surprise when, in his message to Congress of December 8, 1829, President Jackson addressed the problem and sided squarely with white Georgia. But it was of some importance that he devoted so large a portion of his message to the removal question.

❋ The condition and ulterior destiny of the Indian Tribes within the limits of some of our States, have become objects of much interest and importance. It has long been the policy of Government to introduce among them the arts of civilization, in the hope of gradually reclaiming them from a wandering life. This policy has, however, been coupled with another, wholly incompatible with its success. Professing a desire to civilize and settle them, we have, at the same time, lost no opportunity to purchase their lands, and thrust them further into the wilderness. By this means they have not only been kept in a wandering state, but been led to look upon us as unjust and indifferent to their fate. Thus, though lavish in its expenditures upon the subject, Government has constantly defeated its own policy; and the Indians, in general, receding further and further to the West, have retained their savage habits. A portion, however, of the Southern tribes, having mingled much with the whites, and made some progress in the arts of civilized life, have lately attempted to erect an independent government, within the limits of Georgia and Alabama. These States, claiming to be the only Sovereigns within their territories, extended their laws over the Indians; which induced the latter to call upon the United States for protection.

Under these circumstances, the question presented was, whether the General Government had a right to sustain those people in their pretensions? The Constitution declares, that "no new State shall be formed or erected within the jurisdiction of any other State," without the consent of its legislature. If the General Government is not permitted to tolerate the erection of a confederate State within the territory of one of the members of this Union, against her consent; much less could it allow a foreign and independent government to establish itself there. Georgia became a member of the Confederacy which eventuated in our Federal Union, as a sovereign State, always asserting her claim to certain limits; which having been originally defined in her colonial charter, and subsequently recognised in the treaty of peace, she has ever since continued to enjoy. . . .

Actuated by this view of the subject, I informed the Indians inhabiting parts of Georgia and Alabama, that their attempt to establish an independent government would not be countenanced by the Executive of the United States; and advised them to emigrate beyond the Mississippi, or submit to the laws of those States.

Our conduct towards these people is deeply interesting to our national character. Their present condition, contrasted with what they once were, makes a most powerful appeal to our sympathies. Our ancestors found them the uncontrolled possessors of these vast regions. By persuasion and force, they have been made to retire from river to river, and from mountain to mountain; until some of the tribes have become extinct, and others have left but remnants, to preserve, for a while, their once terrible names. Surrounded by the whites, with their arts of civilization, which, by destroying the resources of the savage, doom him to weakness and decay; the fate of the Mohegan, the Narragansett, and the Delaware, is fast overtaking the Choctaw, the Cherokee, and the Creek. That this fate surely awaits them, if they remain within the limits of the States, does not admit of a doubt. Humanity and national honor demand that every effort should be made to avert so great a calamity. It is too late to inquire whether it was just in the United States to include them and their territory within the bounds of new States whose limits they could control. That step cannot be retraced. A State cannot be dismembered by Congress, or restricted in the exercise of her constitutional power. But the people of those States, and of every State, actuated by feelings of justice and a regard for our national honor, submit to you the interesting question, whether something cannot be done, consistently with the rights of the States, to preserve this much injured race?

As a means of effecting this end, I suggest, for your consideration, the propriety of setting apart an ample district West of the Mississippi, and without the limits of any State or Territory, now formed, to be guarantied to the Indian tribes, as long as they shall occupy it: each tribe having a distinct control over the portion designated for its use. There they may be secured in the enjoyment of governments of their own choice, subject to no other control from the United States than such as may be necessary to preserve peace on the frontier, and between the several tribes. There the benevolent may endeavor to teach them the arts of civilization; and, by promoting union and harmony among them, to raise up an interesting commonwealth, destined to perpetuate the race, and to attest the humanity and justice of this Government.

This emigration should be voluntary: for it would be as cruel as unjust to compel the aborigines to abandon the graves of their fathers, and seek a home in a distant land. But they should be distinctly informed that, if they remain within the limits of the States, they must be subject to their laws. In return for their obedience, as individuals, they will, without doubt, be protected in the enjoyment of those possessions which they have improved by their industry. But it seems to me visionary to suppose, that, in this state of things, claims can be allowed on tracts of country on which they have neither dwelt nor made improvements, merely because they have seem them from the mountain, or passed them in the chace. Submitting to the laws of the States, and receiving, like other citizens, protection in their persons and property, they will, ere long, become merged in the mass of our population.

❖ ❖ ❖

Encouraged by Jackson's support, the Georgia Legislature passed a law requiring all white residents of the Cherokee lands to take an oath of allegiance to the state. A New England missionary, Samuel A. Worcester refused. He was arrested, convicted, and sentenced to four years at hard labor. Worcester appealed and John Marshall's Supreme Court ruled that his imprisonment was illegal because the state of Georgia had no such authority within what, by valid treaty with the federal government, was a "domestic, independent nation." In response to this ruling Jackson was alleged to have said, "John Marshall has made his opinion, now let him enforce it."

Georgia refused to abide by Marshall's order, and the president was as good as his word. Although truculently a nationalist in other matters, Jackson's belief that the Indian and white races could not live side by side was so compelling that he was willing to ignore Georgia's defiance of the Supreme Court. Instead, in his Seventh Annual Message to Congress on December 7, 1835, he substantially repeated the sentiments he had expressed in 1829.

Whigs of the era, and many historians since, criticized Jackson's Indian policy as a combination of greed and cynicism. They pointed out that he took an almost diametrically opposing view of "state sovereignty" in his threat to lead an army into South Carolina for that state's refusal to obey a law of Congress.

Jackson *was* inconsistent. Certainly, his passions enabled him to side with Georgia in the matter of removal. But it is also possible to read in his policy a straightforward, melancholy, and regretful resignation to the inevitable. There is even a certain ambivalence towards the march of economic and social progress as Jackson saw it. If Jackson had been sanctimonious in other matters, it would be easier to write off his comments on Indian Removal as hypocrisy. But deviousness and cant were not among Old Hickory's failings. He was blunt, even simple of mind. His weapon was the cudgel held in plain view and not the stiletto secreted in a cuff.

In truth, the state of Georgia was going to have its way with the Cherokee, one way or the other, sooner or later, no matter what stand Jackson might have taken in 1829 or 1835. Throughout American history, the "Indian Question" was resolved in as inevitable a manner as any historical consequence may be said to have been inevitable: triumph of the dynamic mainstream society over the ways of peripheral, even incidental, cultures.

This observation is demonstrated by the fact that the two best-intentioned Congressional formulations of Indian policy, the Dawes Severalty Act of 1887 and the Indian Reorganization Act of 1934, as well as the Alaskan Native Claims Settlement Act of our own era, failed to avert in the slightest the disintegration of Native American cultures. In fact they accelerated it in every case.

2

Henry Clay

❁ ❁ ❁

The American System
1830

"*E*loquence," observed the
philosopher George Santayana, "is a republican art, as conversation
is an aristocratic one." Thomas Jefferson, a brilliant conversationalist
and correspondent, had stammered so badly that he sent his messages
to Congress by courier. The hero of the more democratic politics of
the nineteenth century, however, was the spellbinding orator, who
attracted crowds eager to hear him declaim the values of his community
or his party in delectably fine words and stirring sentiments. He made
nineteenth-century politics the public's most absorbing spectator sport.

Among the acclaimed public speakers of the age, a disproportionate
number were members of the Whig party, including Henry Clay of
Kentucky. Clay could hold the rapt attention of Congress with speeches
that sometimes lasted three days, while ladies in the packed galleries
sucked oranges passed up to them by the crowd of gentlemen below. Of
all nineteenth-century Americans who were never elected president, Clay
probably most deserved to be. He ran for the office five times and came
within a whisker of winning twice. But Clay, like his party, was unlucky.
Despite the fact that the two parties were unusually evenly balanced, Whigs
won only two of the seven presidential elections in which they ran. And
both victorious Whig candidates died, within months of their election,
from exposure to the elements while listening to long speeches.

THE AMERICAN SYSTEM   Speech at Cincinnati, Ohio, August 3, 1830. From *Life and
Speeches of the Hon. Henry Clay*, ed. Daniel Mallory (New York: A. S. Barnes, 1857), I,
647–67.

Of the two parties, the Whigs were the more optimistic. Someone has said that Whigs appealed to the hopes of Americans, while Democrats appealed to their fears. The two Whig presidents convened special sessions to lay before Congress major legislative programs. The Democratic presidents were better known for their vetoes.

Congress, however, was often in Whig hands, where Clay and other members of his party sought to defend and expand a program of national improvements—including the national bank, public works, and protective tariffs—enacted between 1816 and 1828. Clay called it "the American System," and the tariffs were its most important feature. Intended to protect infant industries, they had first been proposed by Alexander Hamilton for nationalistic purposes, to permit the United States to industrialize in the face of superior British competition. The Whigs were nationalists too, but they emphasized the democratic benefits of industrialization. So long as the United States remained wholly agricultural, they said, it would be a commercial colony of Britain, its citizens denied the rich opportunities for varied careers possessed by British subjects. They would be condemned to farm labor, the low productivity of which would leave them little to show for their efforts and little scope for their varied talents. Industrial society, as the British example showed, was culturally as well as materially richer.

In 1830, when he delivered the following address at Cincinnati, Henry Clay was at the midpoint of his long career. He had been in Congress for most of the previous twenty-five years, twelve of them as Speaker of the House. He had just served as Secretary of State under John Quincy Adams. Ahead lay another twenty years in the Senate and as the standard-bearer of the Whig party which he had helped to create. As he had often done before, and would often do again, he defended the "American System" against its Democratic critics in the White House.

❀ With respect to the American system, . . . its great object is to secure the independence of our country, to augment its wealth, and to diffuse the comforts of civilization throughout society. That object, it has been supposed, can be best accomplished by introducing, encouraging, and protecting the arts[1] among us. . . . It is a system which develops, improves, and perfects the capabilities of

---

[1]Mechanical arts or manufacturing.

our common country and enables us to avail ourselves of all the resources with which Providence has blest us. . . . It adds power and strength to our union by new ties of interest, blending and connecting together all its parts in creating an interest with each in the prosperity of the whole. It secures to our own country, whose skill and enterprise . . . cannot be surpassed, those vast profits which are made in other countries by . . . converting the raw material into manufactured articles. . . .

That system has had a wonderful success. It has more than realized all the hopes of its founders. It has completely falsified all the predictions of its opponents. It has increased the wealth, and power, and population of the nation. It has diminished the price of articles of consumption and has placed them within the reach of a far greater number of our people than could have found means to command them if they had been manufactured abroad instead of at home.

But it is useless to dwell on the argument in support of this beneficent system before this audience. It will be of more consequence here to examine some of the objections which are still urged against it and the means which are proposed to subvert it. These objections are now principally confined to its operation upon the great staple of cotton, . . . and they are urged with most vehemence in a particular state.[2] If the objections are well founded, the system should be modified. . . . If they are not, . . . it is to be hoped they will be finally abandoned. . . .

If the cotton planter have any just complaint against the expediency of the American system, it must be founded on the fact that he either sells *less* of his staple, or sells at *lower* prices, or purchases for consumption, articles at *dearer* rates, or of *worse* qualities, in consequence of that system, than he would do if it did not exist. . . .

As respects the sale of his staple, . . . it could be of no advantage to the cotton planter if all the cotton now manufactured both in Europe and America was manufactured exclusively in Europe, and an amount of cotton fabrics should be brought back from Europe equal to both what is now brought from there and what is manufactured in the United States together. Whilst he would gain nothing, the United States would lose the profit and employment

---

[2]A year and a half earlier, angered by the federal tariff of 1828, the South Carolina Legislature had published its *Exposition and Protest*, proclaiming the right of individual states to declare laws of Congress unconstitutional within their borders. In 1832 South Carolina actually tried to carry out this threat of "nullification."

resulting from the manufacture of that portion which is now wrought up by the manufacturers of the United States.

Unless, therefore, it can be shown that, by the reduction of import duties and the overthrow of the American system and by limiting the manufacture of cotton to Europe, a greater amount of the raw material would be consumed than is at present, it is difficult to see what interest . . . the cotton planter has in the subversion of that system. . . .

Upon the supposition just made, of a restriction to Europe of the manufacture of cotton, would more or less of the article be consumed than now is? . . . It is confidently believed that the consumption of cotton fabrics, on the supposition which has been made, within the United States would be much less than it is at present. It would be less, because the American consumer would not possess the means or ability to purchase as much of the European fabric as he now does to buy the American. . . . The establishment of manufactures within the United States enables the manufacturer to sell to the farmer, the mechanic, the physician, the lawyer, and all who are engaged in other pursuits of life; and these, in their turns, supply the manufacturer with . . . whatever . . . his wants require. . . . These mutual exchanges, so animating and invigorating to the industry of the people of the United States, could not possibly be effected between America and Europe if the latter enjoyed the monopoly of manufacturing.

It results, therefore, that, so far as the sale of the great Southern staple is concerned, a greater quantity is sold and consumed, and consequently better prices are obtained, under the operation of the American system than would be without it.

Does that system oblige the cotton planter to buy dearer or worse articles of consumption than he could purchase if it did not exist?

The same cause of American and European competition . . . also enables him to buy cheaper and better articles for consumption. It cannot be doubted that the tendency of the competition between the European and American manufacturer is to reduce the price and improve the quality of their respective fabrics,[3] whenever they come into collision. This is the immutable law of all competition. . . . That the effect of competition between the European and American manufacture has been to supply the American consumer with cheaper and better articles, since the adoption of the American

---

[3]Anything fabricated or manufactured.

system, . . . is incontestable. Both the freeman and slave are now better and cheaper supplied than they were prior to the existence of that system. Cotton fabrics have diminished in price, and been improved in their texture, to an extent that it is difficult for the imagination to keep pace with. . . . The same observation is applicable to those which are exclusively wrought of wool, iron, or glass. In short, it is believed that there is not one item of the tariff inserted for the protection of native industry which has not fallen in price. . . .

Of what then can the South Carolina planter justly complain in the operation of this system? What is there in it which justifies the harsh and strong epithets which some of her politicians have applied to it? . . .

She is oppressed by a great reduction in the price of manufactured articles of consumption.

She is oppressed by the advantage of two markets for the sale of her valuable staple and for the purchase of objects required by her wants.

She is oppressed by better prices for that staple than she could command if the system to which they object did not exist.

She is oppressed by the option of purchasing cheaper and better articles, the produce of the hands of American freemen, instead of dearer and worse articles, the produce of the hands of British subjects.

She is oppressed by the measures of a government in which she has had, for many years, a larger proportion of power and influence . . . than any state in the whole Union in comparison with the population. . . .

The government of the United States, at this juncture, exhibits a most remarkable spectacle. *It is that of a majority of the nation having put the powers of government into the hands of the minority.* If anyone can doubt this, let him look back at the elements of the executive,[4] at the presiding officers of the two houses, at the composition and the chairmen of the most important committees, who shape and direct the public business of Congress. Let him look, above all, *at measures*, the necessary consequences of such an anomalous state of things— internal improvements gone, or going; the whole American system threatened, and the triumphant shouts of anticipated victory sounding in our ears. Georgia, extorting from the fears of an af-

---

[4]Andrew Jackson had been inaugurated president the year before. John Calhoun of South Carolina, author of the nullification doctrine, was vice-president.

frighted majority of Congress an Indian bill,[5] which may prostrate all the laws, treaties, and policy which have regulated our relations with the Indians from the commencement of our government. And politicians in South Carolina, at the same time, brandishing the torch of civil war and pronouncing unbounded eulogiums upon the President, for the good he has done and the still greater good which they expect at his hands, and the sacrifice of the interests of the majority. . . .

Another mode of destroying the system, . . . which its foes have adopted, is to assail the character of its friends. Can you otherwise account for the spirit of animosity with which I am pursued? A sentiment this morning caught my eye, in the shape of a Fourth of July toast, proposed . . . in South Carolina, by a gentleman whom I never saw and to whom I am a total stranger. With humanity, charity, and Christian benevolence unexampled, he wished that I might be driven so far beyond the frigid regions of the northern zone that all hell could not thaw me! Do you believe it was against *me*, this feeble and frail form, tottering with age, this lump of perishing clay, that all this kindness was directed? No, no, no. It was against the measures of policy which I have espoused, against the system which I have labored to uphold, that it was aimed. If I had been opposed to the tariff, and internal improvements, and in favor of the South Carolina doctrine of nullification, the same worthy gentleman would have wished that I might be ever fanned by soft breezes, . . . that my path might be strewed with roses, and my abode be an earthly paradise.

I am now a private man, the humblest of the humble, possessed of no office, no power, . . . no official corps to chant my praises and to drink, in flowing bowls, my health and prosperity. . . . Why then am I thus pursued, my words perverted and distorted, my acts misrepresented? . . . It is not against me. That is impossible. A few years more, and this body will be where all is still and silent. It is against the principles of civil liberty, against the tariff and internal improvements, to which the better part of my life has been devoted, that this implacable war is waged. My enemies flatter themselves that those systems may be overthrown by my destruction. Vain and impotent hope! My existence is not of the smallest conse-

---

[5]In 1830 Congress gave President Jackson the Indian Removal Bill that he had requested (see reading 1 above). Clay was virtually the only western statesman to protest, even though his own constituents in Kentucky scarcely supported his views. His speech in the Senate in 1835, denouncing the brutal treatment of the Indians, "drew tears from the eyes of the senators," in the words of one historian, but, alas, little else.

quence to their preservation. They will survive me. Long, long after I am gone, . . . whilst truth shall hold its sway among men, those systems will invigorate the industry and animate the hopes of the farmer, the mechanic, the manufacturer, and all other classes of our countrymen.

❄ ❄ ❄

In the long run Whig tariff policy won out. During the nineteenth century the United States industrialized behind very high tariff walls which ranged from 20 percent of the value of protected commodities in 1816 to more than 50 percent by the end of the century. Only between 1846 and 1860 did Democratic opposition manage temporarily to bring tariffs down. In 1861, however, the Republican party, which succeeded the Whigs, restored tariff protection and continued to do so in every Republican administration down to Herbert Hoover's. Only in the mid-twentieth century, long after it had become the leading industrial power in the world, did the United States rather belatedly dismantle its tariff barriers. Since 1934 the average tariff has been reduced from 60 percent to 9 percent at the conclusion of the "Kennedy Round" of tariff revisions in 1973.

Abraham Lincoln, who signed the high Morrill Tariff in 1861, illustrates the persistence of Whig ideals in the new Republican party. Lincoln had been a lifelong Whig, who once called Henry Clay "my beau ideal of a statesman." "During my whole political life," Lincoln said, "I have loved and revered him as a teacher and leader." Lincoln's own bleak youth on frontier farms led him to cast a cold eye on any attempt to idealize agrarian life. He clearly regarded his boyhood circumstances as narrow, stultifying, and culturally as well as materially impoverished. The millions of Americans who during the nineteenth century fled the farms on which they had been born for the nation's growing cities probably agreed.

3

Andrew Jackson
❁ ❁ ❁

Veto of the Bank Renewal Bill
1832

*I*n 1787 the Constitution made the nation's money supply the exclusive responsibility of federal officials, who promptly erected a mint at Philadelphia and began to strike gold and silver coins bearing the American eagle. By the time of the Civil War the nation's supply of money had increased fortyfold, from perhaps $15 million to about $600 million. Only a fourth of it, however, was official coin. The actual money supply of the country had become privately printed paper, produced by a wonderful new technique the American people had discovered outside the Constitution—banking.

Banks create money. A banker knows that it is unlikely that every depositor will want all his money back at the same time. Experience has taught him that it is usually safe to keep only about a quarter of his deposits on hand to meet day-to-day demands, and that he can earn profits on the rest by investing it, instead of leaving it to lie idle in his vaults. Therefore, when a depositor gives him $100, he will probably loan $75 of it to someone else, usually a businessman needing extra cash for a month or two. Now the banker's books show $100 credited to the depositor *and* $75 credited to the borrower, or a total of $175. In fact, before the depositor eventually asks for his $100 back, several banks, acting one after another, may have

VETO OF THE BANK RENEWAL BILL   Veto Message, July 10, 1832. From *A Compilation of the Messages and Papers of the Presidents*, ed. James D. Richardson (Washington: U.S. Government Printing Office, 1896–99), II, 576–90.

multiplied it into as much as $400. The whole purpose of banking is to make money by making money.

The banker's skillful juggling act benefits others besides himself. Because he can pay interest to depositors, he attracts savings. Unlike the supply of gold and silver, which is fixed, bank money can be made to expand or contract to meet the seasonal needs of trade. The credit which the banker extends to businessmen permits them to anticipate future earnings and put idle resources to work sooner and more efficiently. In all of these ways banks accelerate economic development.

The good done by American banks was clouded during the early nineteenth century, however, by their uneven quality. Many banks, especially in the Northeast, were run as well as any modern bank, and several of them are still doing business today. Others, especially in the West, possessed few assets beyond their extravagant hopes. Like other businesses, banking also attracted its share of racketeers. In general about half of all American banks formed before the Civil War failed. During business depressions the monetary wreckage was terrible. Bankers who had made imprudent loans gazed helplessly at empty vaults; depositors were turned away from tellers' windows empty-handed; businessmen in debt beyond their means faced bankruptcy and foreclosure. At such times chastened Americans recalled Benjamin Franklin's bitter proverb—"He that goes a-borrowing goes a-sorrowing."

Andrew Jackson, who early in life had a very unfortunate run-in with modern credit, hated banks, as did many other old-fashioned Americans. As president he spearheaded an anti-bank movement which ran its course between 1830 and 1845. Jackson's "hard-money" views were supported by most Democrats, while Whigs struggled to defend the nation's progressive banking institutions. Jackson eliminated banking at the federal level altogether. In 1832 he refused to recharter the Bank of the United States which controlled a quarter of the banking assets of the country. By 1835 he had eliminated the national debt as a potential source of banking capital by completely paying it off. Remaining federal funds were snatched from the hands of bankers in 1840 and squirreled away in underground vaults. And after 1836 the federal government refused to conduct its own business in any money but gold and silver. During the 1840s hard-money Democrats in state legislatures forced local banks out of business and in several states used their constitutions to prohibit banking altogether. Everywhere banking capital and credit were sharply reduced, and by 1852 seven of the thirty-one states had no banks at all.

Part of the Democrats' dislike of banking stemmed from their conservative distrust of modern economic devices which few of them (and few Americans today) understood very well. The other part was political. Jackson believed that banks were privileged monopolies which threatened to destroy the republic. Because the early nineteenth century lacked general incorporation laws, bankers needed special legislative enactments before they could open for business. Favoritism was customary, and between businessmen and legislators gifts were freely exchanged. Thus no one was surprised to learn that the two most powerful defenders of the Bank of the United States in the Senate, Daniel Webster and Henry Clay, were also on the Bank's payroll. That was the way it had always been, and that was the way it would always be, the Jacksonians charged, so long as government was involved in the economy. Only by strictly limiting government and divorcing it from business could corruption be avoided. Hence the motto, trumpeted daily in the Jacksonian press, "The world is too much governed."

❁ The bill to modify and continue ... the Bank of the United States was presented to me on the 4th July instant. Having considered it with the solemn regard to the principles of the Constitution which the day was calculated to inspire, and come to the conclusion that it ought not to become a law, I herewith return it to the Senate ... with my objections. ...

I sincerely regret that in the act before me I can perceive none of those modifications of the bank charter which are necessary, in my opinion, to make it compatible with justice, with sound policy, or with the Constitution of our country. ...

The Bank of the United States will have existed at the time this act is intended to take effect, twenty years. It enjoys an exclusive privilege of banking under the authority of the General Government,[1] a monopoly of its favor and support, and, as a necessary consequence, almost a monopoly of the foreign and domestic exchange. The powers, privileges, and favors bestowed upon it in the original charter, by increasing the value of the stock far above its par value, [have] operated as a gratuity of many millions to the stockholders. ...

The act before me proposes another gratuity to the holders of the same stock ... of at least seven million more. ... It is not our own citizens only who are to receive the bounty of our Government. More than eight millions of the stock of this bank are held by foreigners.[2] By this act the American Republic proposes virtually to make them a present of some millions of dollars. For these gratuities

---

[1]Federal government.

[2]Almost all foreign shareholders in the Bank were British.

to foreigners and to some of our own opulent citizens the act secures no equivalent whatever. . . .

It is not conceivable how the present stockholders can have any claim to the special favor of the Government. . . . This act does not permit competition in the purchase of this monopoly. It seems to be predicated on the erroneous idea that the present stockholders have a prescriptive right not only to the favor but to the bounty of Government. . . . For their benefit does this act exclude the whole American people from competition in the purchase of this monopoly and dispose of it for many millions less than it is worth. . . .

If our Government must sell monopolies, it would seem to be its duty to take nothing less than their full value, and if gratuities must be made once in fifteen or twenty years, let them not be bestowed on the subjects of a foreign government nor upon a designated and favored class of men in our own country. It is but justice and good policy, as far as the nature of the case will admit, to confine our favors to our own fellow-citizens, and let each in his turn enjoy an opportunity to profit by our bounty. In the bearings of the act before me upon these points I find ample reasons why it should not become a law. . . .

Is there no danger to our liberty and independence in a bank that in its nature has so little to bind it to our country? . . . Should its influence become concentered . . . in the hands of a self-elected directory whose interests are identified with those of the foreign stockholders, will there not be cause to tremble for the purity of our elections in peace and for the independence of our country in war? . . . Should the stock of the bank principally pass into the hands of the subjects of a foreign country, and we should unfortunately become involved in a war with that country, what would be our condition? . . .

If we must have a bank with private stockholders, every consideration of sound policy and every impulse of American feeling admonishes that it should be *purely American*. Its stockholders should be composed exclusively of our own citizens, who at least ought to be friendly to our Government and willing to support it in times of difficulty and danger. . . .

It is maintained by the advocates of the bank that its constitutionality . . . ought to be considered as settled by precedent and by the decision of the Supreme Court. To this conclusion I cannot assent. Mere precedent is a dangerous source of authority, and should not be regarded as deciding questions of constitutional power except where the acquiescence of the people and the States can be considered as well settled. . . .

[Even] if the opinion of the Supreme Court covered the whole ground of this act, it ought not to control the coordinate authorities of this Government. The Congress, the Executive, and the Court must each for itself be guided by its own opinion of the Constitution. Each public officer who takes an oath to support the Constitution swears that he will support it as he understands it, and not as it is understood by others. . . . The opinion of the judges has no more authority over Congress than the opinion of Congress has over the judges, and on that point the President is independent of both. . . .

It is maintained by some that the bank is a means of executing the constitutional power "to coin money and regulate the value thereof." Congress have established a mint to coin money and passed laws to regulate the value thereof. The money so coined, with its value so regulated, and such foreign coins as Congress may adopt are the only currency known to the Constitution. But if they have other power to regulate the currency, it was conferred to be exercised by themselves, and not to be transferred to a corporation. If the bank be established for that purpose, with a charter unalterable without its consent, Congress have parted with their power for a term of years, during which the Constitution is a dead letter. It is neither necessary nor proper to transfer its legislative power to such a bank, and therefore unconstitutional. . . .

Considered in connection with the decision of the Supreme Court,[3] . . . this act takes from the States the power to tax a portion of the banking business carried on within their limits, in subversion of one of the strongest barriers which secured them against Federal encroachments. . . . It may be safely assumed that none of those sages who had an agency in forming or adopting our Constitution ever imagined that any portion of the taxing power of the States not prohibited to them nor delegated to Congress was to be swept away and annihilated as a means of executing certain powers delegated to Congress.

If our power over means is so absolute that the Supreme Court will not call in question the constitutionality of an act of Congress the subject of which "is not prohibited, and is really calculated to effect any of the objects intrusted to the Goverment," although, as in the case before me, it takes away powers expressly granted to

---

[3]Jackson refers specifically to the case of *McCulloch* v. *Maryland* (1819) in which the Supreme Court affirmed the constitutionality of the Bank of the United States under the authority of Congress in the Constitution "to make all laws which shall be necessary and proper for carrying into execution" its delegated powers. Chief Justice John Marshall had held, therefore, that as an agency of the federal government the Bank could not be taxed as an ordinary business by state legislatures, some of which had attempted to drive it out of business by prohibitive levies.

Congress and rights scrupulously reserved to the States, it becomes us to proceed in our legislation with the utmost caution. Though not directly, our own powers and the rights of the States may be indirectly legislated away in the use of means to execute substantive powers. . . . Thus may our own powers and the rights of the States . . . be frittered away and extinguished in the use of means employed by us to execute other powers. . . .

It is to be regretted that the rich and powerful too often bend the acts of government to their selfish purposes. Distinctions in society will always exist under every just government. Equality of talents, of education, or of wealth cannot be produced by human institutions. In the full enjoyment of the gifts of Heaven and the fruits of superior industry, economy, and virtue, every man is equally entitled to protection by law. But when the laws undertake to add to these natural and just advantages artificial distinctions— to grant titles, gratuities, and exclusive privileges, to make the rich richer and the potent more powerful—[then] the humble members of society, the farmers, mechanics, and laborers, who have neither the time nor the means of securing like favors to themselves, have a right to complain of the injustice of their Government.

There are no necessary evils in government. Its evils exist only in its abuses. If it would confine itself to equal protection, and, as Heaven does its rains, shower its favors alike on the high and the low, the rich and the poor, it would be an unqualified blessing. In the act before me there seems to be a wide and unnecessary departure from these principles.

Nor is our Government to be maintained or our Union preserved by invasions of the rights and powers of the several States. In thus attempting to make our General Government strong we make it weak. Its true strength consists in leaving individuals and States as much as possible to themselves—in making itself felt, not in its power, but in its beneficence; not in its control, but in its protection; not in binding the States more closely to the center, but leaving each to move unobstructed in its proper orbit.

❋ ❋ ❋

America's flirtation with a bankless future was very brief. So quixotic a crusade stood no chance of success in a country which was industrializing hand over fist. Nor can we say it did very much to make the nation's banking institutions any sounder. During the 1850s economic recovery spurred a demand for credit which permanently overwhelmed

the hard-money position. "What we want is more money," cried Colonel
Mulberry Sellers in Mark Twain's *The Gilded Age*, and most Americans
agreed. There followed a curious compromise. Whigs, who wanted banks,
gave up the cause of chartered monopolies. Democrats, who hated
monopoly, gave up the cause of hard money. Each party salvaged half its
program and produced, in state after state during the 1850s, "free-
banking" measures which permitted any businessmen who so desired to
set up in banking. The result was permanently inflationary. In the words
of one scholar, Americans, forced to choose the lesser of two evils, had
concluded that "too much money was better than not enough."

Thus the more enduring legacy of the Jacksonians came to be not
hard money, but the destruction of monopoly privilege and the
democratization of business opportunity. Jackson had carried his crusade
against corruption even into the federal bureaucracy. Political appointees
who had made lifetime careers of feeding at the public trough were
turned into the street. "The duties of all public officers are . . . so plain
and simple that men of intelligence may readily qualify for their
performance," said Jackson as he announced the principle of "rotation in
office." Again the results were mixed. Shortly thereafter one of Jackson's
own appointees became the first man ever to steal more than a million
dollars from the United States government. Within a decade the wholesale
buying up of legislatures by railroad promoters, which formed so
conspicuous a feature of the years following the Civil War, had already
begun. The leading historian of our public service laments that under the
Jacksonians "standards of official conduct . . . were . . . regrettably inferior
to those which had been nurtured and protected by Federalists and
Republicans alike." This is too short-sighted a view. The bacchanalia of
corruption in mid-nineteenth-century America, which the Jacksonians
helped to introduce, may even have been a step forward: it was
competitive. In place of the elite patronage and favoritism of the past, it
substituted the wide-open, free-swinging corruption of the marketplace.
Equality of opportunity applies to crooks too.

4

John L. O'Sullivan

❖ ❖ ❖

Manifest Destiny
1845

*B*efore the second half of the
nineteenth century the eventual boundaries of the United States were
anybody's guess. North, south, and west of the new republic lay millions
of square miles of wilderness. These lands were claimed by the various
European powers, but poorly occupied by them and only sparsely
inhabited by Indians and frontier drifters. By all the standards which had
applied since the settlement of the first colonies, the land would eventually
come into the possession of whoever could effectively occupy it.

The people of the United States, rapidly increasing and economically
advanced, were the likeliest candidates. Even without the intervention of
their government, the more productive uses to which American settlers put
their land made it more valuable to them than to its original inhabitants. If
nothing else, simple purchase would someday effect the conquest of the
continent. Thus Secretary of State John Quincy Adams observed to the
cabinet in 1819 that "Our proper dominion [is] the continent of North
America, . . . not [from] any spirit of encroachment or ambition on our
part, . . . but because it is a physical, moral, and political absurdity that . . .
fragments of territory, . . . worthless and burdensome to their owners,
should exist permanently contiguous to a great, powerful, enterprising,
and rapidly-growing nation."

Once settlement had reached the Ohio Valley in the 1790s, the
Mississippi River was no longer an adequate western boundary. A river is

MANIFEST DESTINY   From "Annexation," *The United States Magazine and Democratic
Review*, XVII (July 1845), 6–14.

not a barrier but an invitation to travel, and control of the great waterway was vital to western farmers who used it to float their crops to market. It was because of the river that Jefferson had purchased Louisiana in 1803. In 1819 his successors negotiated a comprehensive treaty with Spain, acquiring Florida and fixing the frontiers of the nation along the western edge of Louisiana at the natural barrier of the Rocky Mountains. Here President Monroe was satisfied expansion should cease. He believed that if, someday, American settlement should cross the Rockies and reach the Pacific, a separate American republic should be established there. Senator Benton even proposed erecting on the highest peak of the Continental Divide a statue of the great god Terminus.

So matters stood until the 1840s when even the terms of the question were changed by a wave of exuberant expansionism whipped up within the Democratic party. In the course of a few years Andrew Jackson's successors added another million square miles to the United States and pushed its boundaries to the Pacific, not by peaceful occupation but by military force against the newly independent Republic of Mexico, which was despoiled of a third of its territory. The expansionism of the 1840s was less an expression of American nationalism than of partisanship and sectionalism. Its strongest appeal was to the restless population of the southwestern frontier and to those southerners who saw in territorial expansion a program for the salvation of slavery and the extension of states' rights. President James K. Polk, who was elected on an expansionist platform in 1844, would have liked peace, but he wanted California more. Unable to persuade the Mexicans to sell it, he forced a conflict with them over the disputed boundary of Texas in 1846.

A year earlier the term "Manifest Destiny" had been coined by a New York newspaper editor, John L. O'Sullivan, a Democrat whose expansionism was both boundless and indiscriminate. "Texas . . . is secure," he cried in 1845, "and so now, as the Razor Strop man says, 'Who's the next customer?' Shall it be California or Canada?" As soon as the war with Mexico began O'Sullivan demanded California for an indemnity. When victorious American troops occupied Mexico City, he (and several members of Polk's cabinet) called for the annexation of all Mexico. Polk was more cautious and settled for California. But during the 1850s, under presidents Pierce and Buchanan, expansionist projects proliferated along the southern borders of the United States. In 1850 an army of volunteers recruited from the lower Mississippi Valley invaded Cuba with the assistance of Governor Quitman of Mississippi. In 1854 several of Pierce's diplomats in Europe threatened Spain with war unless Cuba were sold to the United States. In 1858 Senator Houston of Texas introduced a bill to establish a protectorate over Mexico, a measure supported by extreme southern sectionalists like Robert Toombs and George Fitzhugh. Only the outbreak of the Civil War forced a halt. O'Sullivan (whom Pierce made ambassador to Portugal) participated in several of these ventures. When the Civil War began he sided with the Confederacy.

❀ It is time now for opposition to the Annexation of Texas[1] to cease, all further agitation of the waters of bitterness and strife, at least in connexion with this question,—even though it may perhaps be required of us as a necessary condition of the freedom of our institutions, that we must live on for ever in a state of unpausing struggle and excitement upon some subject of party division or other. But, in regard to Texas, enough has now been given to Party. It is time for the common duty of Patriotism to the Country to succeed;—or if this claim will not be recognized, it is at least time for common sense to acquiesce with decent grace in the inevitable and the irrevocable.

Texas is now ours. Already, before these words are written, her Convention has undoubtedly ratified the acceptance, by her Congress, of our proffered invitation into the Union; and made the requisite changes in her already republican form of constitution to adopt it to its future federal relations. Her star and her stripe may already be said to have taken their place in the glorious blazon of our common nationality; and the sweep of our eagle's wing already includes within its circuit the wide extent of her fair and fertile land. She is no longer to us a mere geographical space—a certain combination of coast, plain, mountain, valley, forest and stream. She is no longer to us a mere country on the map. She comes within the dear and sacred designation of Our Country; no longer a "*pays*,"[2] she is a part of "*la patrie*";[3] and that which is at once a sentiment and a virtue, Patriotism, already begins to thrill for her too within the national heart. . . .

Why, were other reasoning wanting, in favor of now elevating this question of the reception of Texas into the Union, out of the lower region of our past party dissensions, up to its proper level of a high and broad nationality, it surely is to be found, found abundantly, in the manner in which other nations[4] have undertaken to intrude themselves into it, between us and the proper parties to the case, in a spirit of hostile interference against us, for the avowed object of thwarting our policy and hampering our power, limiting our greatness and checking the fulfilment of our manifest destiny

---

[1]Four months earlier the Texas Republic had been annexed to the United States by Congressional joint resolution (March 1, 1845), but only after bitter partisan controversy.

[2]French for land or region.

[3]French for fatherland.

[4]O'Sullivan names England "our old rival and enemy." The British, who had appointed themselves the anti-slavery policeman of the world, had used their influence to obstruct the development of a new slave state in Texas.

to overspread the continent allotted by Providence for the free development of our yearly multiplying millions. . . .

It is wholly untrue, and unjust to ourselves, the pretence that the Annexation has been a measure of spoliation, unrightful and unrighteous—of military conquest under forms of peace and law—of territorial aggrandizement at the expense of justice, and justice due by a double sanctity to the weak. . . . If Texas became peopled with an American population, it was by no contrivance of our government, but on the express invitation of that of Mexico herself; accompanied with such guaranties of State independence, and the maintenance of a federal system analogous to our own, as constituted a compact fully justifying the strongest measure of redress on the part of those afterwards deceived in this guaranty, and sought to be enslaved under the yoke imposed by its violation. She was released, rightfully and absolutely released, from all Mexican allegiance, or duty of cohesion to the Mexican political body, by the acts and fault of Mexico herself, and Mexico alone.[5] There never was a clearer case. . . .

Nor is there any just foundation of the charge that Annexation is a great pro-slavery measure—calculated to increase and perpetuate that institution. Slavery had nothing to do with it. . . . The country which was the subject of Annexation in this case, happens to be—or rather the portion of it now actually settled, happens to be—a slave country. But a similar process might have taken place in proximity to a different section of our Union; and indeed there is a great deal of Annexation yet to take place, within the life of the present generation, along the whole line of our northern border. Texas has been absorbed into the Union in the inevitable fulfilment of the general law which is rolling our population westward; the connexion of which with that ratio of growth in population which is destined within a hundred years to swell our numbers to the enormous population of *two hundred and fifty millions* (if not more), is too evident to leave us in doubt of the manifest design of Providence in regard to the occupation of this continent. . . .

California will, probably, next fall away from the loose adhesion which, in such a country as Mexico, holds a remote province in a slight equivocal kind of dependence on the metropolis. Imbecile and distracted, Mexico never can exert any real governmental authority over such a country. The impotence of the one and the distance of the other, must make the relation one of virtual inde-

---

[5]The Texans won their independence from Mexico in 1836.

pendence; unless, by stunting the province of all natural growth, and forbidding that immigration which can alone develop its capabilities and fulfil the purposes of its creation, tyranny may retain a military dominion which is no government in the legitimate sense of the term. In the case of California this is now impossible. The Anglo-Saxon foot is already on its borders. Already the advance guard of the irresistable army of Anglo-Saxon emigration has begun to pour down upon it, armed with the plough and the rifle, and marking its trail with schools and colleges, courts and representative halls, mills and meeting-houses. A population will soon be in actual occupation of California, over which it will be idle for Mexico to dream of dominion. They will necessarily become independent. All this without agency of our government, without responsibility of our people—in the natural flow of events, the spontaneous working of principles, and the adaptation of the tendencies and wants of the human race to the elemental circumstances in the midst of which they find themselves placed. . . .

Away, then, with all idle French talk of *balances of power* on the American Continent. There is no growth in Spanish America! Whatever progress of population there may be in the British Canadas, is only for their own early severance of their present colonial relation to the little island three thousand miles across the Atlantic; soon to be followed by Annexation, and destined to swell the still accumulating momentum of our progress. And whatsoever may hold the balance, though they should cast into the opposite scale all the bayonets and cannon, not only of France and England, but of Europe entire, how would it kick the beam against the simple solid weight of the two hundred and fifty or three hundred millions— and American millions—destined to gather beneath the flutter of the stripes and stars, in the fast hastening year of the Lord 1945?[6]

❀ ❀ ❀

The war with Mexico was more bitterly opposed than any American war before Vietnam. Whigs were very reluctant expansionists at best. Someone has said that while Democrats aimed to expand the quantity of the United States, Whigs hoped to improve its quality. "Opposed to the instinct of boundless acquisition stands that of Internal Improvement," wrote one Whig editor. "A nation cannot simultaneously devote its energies to the absorption of others' territories and the improvement

---

[6]The population of the United States in 1940 was 130 million.

of its own." Senator Webster was even more succinct: "We have a Sparta, embellish it!" In the end both Clay and Webster lost sons in a war which each in his grief believed to have been unnecessary and unjust.

By this time thoughtful northerners were alarmed by the inability of the United States to rid itself of the lawlessness and violence which the Mexican war seemed to exemplify. Violence itself was becoming a sectional issue. More than one northerner who visited the lower South felt that he was "indeed in the land of Lynch-law and bowie-knives, where the passions of men have not yet been subordinated to the influence of the tribunals of justice." The southern origin of the river population made the banks of the Mississippi a line of disorder from New Orleans to Wisconsin. The lower South and Southwest were the last regions in the country to shelter masters flogging slaves, gentlemen duelists, country folk baiting bears and pulling ganders, and members of Congress like Sam Houston, Preston Brooks, and Albert Rust whose notions of parliamentary procedure included physical assaults on other representatives. The Whig goal of improving American morals was especially resented by those Americans whose morals most needed to be improved. Generally they took refuge behind the Democratic doctrines of unfettered individualism and limited government. Thus one historian quotes a frontiersman jailed for manslaughter: "Now-a-days you can't put an inch or so of knife into a fellow . . . but . . . law, law, law is the word. . . . I tell you I won't stay in no such a country. I mean to go to Texas, where a man can have some peace and not be interfered with in his private concerns."

When a pro-southern mob murdered an abolitionist newspaper editor in the river town of Alton, Illinois, in 1837, a young Whig from that state, Abraham Lincoln, prophetically warned that the "increasing disregard for law which pervades the country" is an "ill omen" by which "our political institutions . . . may effectually be broken down and destroyed." In 1861, when he was president and the South had seceded, Lincoln viewed secession as yet another example of habitual southern lawlessness. It is, he said, "the essence of anarchy."

5

Horace Mann

❖ ❖ ❖

Report of the Massachusetts Board of Education

1848

During the Industrial Revolution
Americans learned to increase their economic productivity by investing
in labor-saving machines. Much earlier they had begun to make another
capital investment of equal importance—an investment in the productive
skills of workers. A revolution in education had begun in the Atlantic world
during the colonial period. For the first time in history more than a small
fraction of any population learned to read and write. In medieval England
even aristocrats had been in most cases illiterate. But by the end of the
eighteenth century, in progressive regions like New England and
Scotland, virtually the entire male and about half of the female population
could read.

The schools which produced these results were, by our standards,
very haphazard. As early as 1647 Puritan authorities in Massachusetts had
required all towns in the province to maintain a school, but throughout the
colonial period vague rules were only laxly enforced. The rural district
schools of the northern colonies and the "field schools" of the South were

REPORT OF THE MASSACHUSETTS BOARD OF EDUCATION   From Twelfth Annual
Report, 1848, *Annual Reports on Education* (Boston: Horace B. Fuller, 1868), pp.
650–754.

entirely dependent upon local initiative, support, and direction. Typically as many as 60 or 70 schoolchildren, of every age between two and fourteen, were crowded into single-room schoolhouses erected on the most worthless land frugal authorities could discover. Attendance was wholly voluntary and limited to winter and summer sessions of eight to ten weeks each (most children past the age of ten missed the summer term since their labor was needed in the fields). Schoolmasters, who thus had only part-time work, were at worst alcoholic itinerants, at best young persons only a step ahead of their pupils. Even the most conscientious faced bewildering difficulties in any attempt to introduce order among their ill-assorted students compounded by the cherished custom according to which each family provided its own, different, heirloom textbook. Nowhere were schools supported exclusively, or even primarily, by taxes. Instead families paid tuition, contributed cordwood for the winter, and boarded the unhappy schoolmaster around from household to household. This colonial system of education, probably sufficient to meet the needs of the mostly rural society which it served, persisted long after the American Revolution. American children were being taught in the 1830s much as they had been in the eighteenth century.

A successful movement to provide schools more adequate to the needs of industrial society was one of the most impressive achievements of the years 1830–1860, at least in the northern states. Reformers worked to improve attendance, lengthen the school term, introduce coherently graded schools, and require uniform textbooks. They took steps to make teaching a recognized profession, offering higher wages and longer-term employment, and encouraging the hiring of females trained especially to be teachers at new state normal schools. ("A profession is to be created for women," the feminist Catherine Beecher exulted.) Above all they sought to curtail local independence by the introduction of state supervision and funding, and to compel, by state legislation, the abolition of tuition. Instead schools were to be supported wholly by taxes—paid by parents and non-parents alike.

Horace Mann was a prominent Massachusetts reform politician who, under milestone legislation enacted in 1837, was appointed the nation's first state superintendent of schools. His persuasive annual reports, drafted to mobilize public support for the "common school" ideal, made him the best-known school reformer of his generation.

❁ Without undervaluing any other human agency, it may be safely affirmed that the common school, improved and energized as it can easily be, may become the most effective and benignant[1] of all the forces of civilization. Two reasons sustain this position. In the first place, there is a universality in its operation, which can be affirmed of no other institution whatever. If administered in the spirit of justice and conciliation, all the rising generation may be brought within the circle of its reformatory and elevating influences. And, in the second place, the materials upon which it operates are so pliant and ductile as to be susceptible of assuming a greater variety of forms than any other earthly work of the Creator. . . .

I proceed, then, in endeavoring to show how the true business of the schoolroom connects itself, and becomes identical, with the great interests of society. The former is the infant, immature state of those interests; the latter their developed, adult state. As "the child is father to the man," so may the training of the schoolroom expand into the institution and fortunes of the State. . . .

Intellectual Education

According to the European theory, men are divided into classes— some to toil and earn, others to seize and enjoy. According to the Massachusetts theory, all are to have an equal chance for earning, and equal security in the enjoyment of what they earn. The latter tends to equality of condition; the former, to the grossest inequalities. Tried by any Christian standard of morals, . . . can anyone hesitate, for a moment, in declaring which of the two will produce the greater amount of human welfare? . . .

I suppose it to be the universal sentiment of all those who mingle any ingredient of benevolence with their notions on political economy,[2] that vast and overshadowing private fortunes are among the greatest dangers to which the happiness of the people in a republic can be subjected. Such fortunes would create a feudalism of a new kind, but one more oppressive and unrelenting than that of the middle ages. . . . Now, two or three things will doubtless be

---

[1]Exerting benign influence.
[2]Economics.

admitted to be true, beyond all controversy, in regard to Massachusetts. By its industrial condition, and its business operations, it is exposed, far beyond any other state in the Union, to the fatal extremes of overgrown wealth and desperate poverty. . . .

Now, surely nothing but universal education can counterwork this tendency to the domination of capital and the servility of labor. If one class possesses all the wealth and the education, while the residue of society is ignorant and poor, it matters not by what name the relation between them may be called: the latter, in fact and in truth, will be the servile dependents and subjects of the former. But, if education be equably diffused, it will draw property after it by the strongest of all attractions; for such a thing never did happen, and never can happen, as that an intelligent and practical body of men should be permanently poor. . . . The people of Massachusetts have, in some degree, appreciated the truth, that the unexampled prosperity of the State—its comfort, its competence, its general intelligence and virtue—is attributable to the education, more or less perfect, which all its people have received. . . .

Education, then, beyond all other devices of human origin, is the great equalizer of the conditions of men—the balance-wheel of the social machinery. . . . It gives each man the independence and the means by which he can resist the selfishness of other men. It does better than to disarm the poor of their hostility towards the rich: it prevents being poor. . . .

In this fact, then, we find a solution of the problem that so long embarrassed inquirers. The reason why the mechanical and useful arts—those arts which have done so much to civilize mankind, and which have given comforts and luxuries to the common laborer of the present day, such as kings and queens could not command three centuries ago—the reason why these arts made no progress . . . until recently . . . is that the labor of the world was performed by ignorant men. . . . But just in proportion as intelligence—that is, education—has quickened and stimulated a greater and a greater number of minds, just in the same proportion have inventions and discoveries increased in their wonderfulness. . . .

For the creation of wealth, then—for the existence of a wealthy people and a wealthy nation—intelligence is the grand condition. The number of improvers will increase as the intellectual constituency, if I may call it, increases. . . . Let this development proceed, and contributions, numberless, and of inestimable value, will be sure to follow. That political economy, therefore, which busies itself about capital and labor, supply and demand, interest and rents, favorable and unfavorable balances of trade, but leaves out of account the element of a widespread mental development, is nought but stupendous folly. The greatest of all the arts in political economy is to change a consumer into a producer; and the next greatest is to increase the producer's producing power—an end to be directly attained by increasing his intelligence. . . .

Political Education

A republican form of government, without intelligence in the people, must be, on a vast scale, what a mad-house without superintendent or keepers would be on a small one. . . . However elevated the moral character of a constituency may be, however well informed in matters of general science or history, yet they must, if citizens of a republic, understand something of the true nature and functions of the government under which they live. . . . In all nations, hardly excepting the most rude and barbarous, the future sovereign receives some training which is supposed to fit him for the exercise of the . . . duties of his anticipated station. . . . Then surely, it would be . . . a proof of . . . barbarism amongst us to empower any individual to use the elective franchise without preparing him for so momentous a trust. Hence the Constitution of the United States, and of our own State, should be made a study in our public schools. . . .

Had the obligation of the future citizen been sedulously inculcated upon all the children of this Republic, would the patriot have had to mourn over so many instances where the voter, not being able to accomplish his purpose by voting, has proceeded to accomplish it by violence? . . . If the responsibleness and value of the elective franchise were duly appreciated, . . . no man would throw away his vote through caprice or wantonness, any more than he would throw away his estate, or sell his family into bondage. . . .

The establishment of a republican government, without well-appointed and efficient means for the universal education of the people, is the most rash and foolhardy experiment ever tried by man. . . . It may be an easy thing to make a republic, but it is a very laborious thing to make republicans; and woe to the republic that rests upon no better foundations than ignorance, selfishness, and passion! . . .

Moral Education

Moral education is a primal necessity of social existence. The unrestrained passions of men are not only homicidal, but suicidal; and a community without a conscience would soon extinguish itself. . . . To all doubters, disbelievers, or despairers in human progress, it may still be said, there is one experiment which has never yet been tried. . . . It is expressed in these few and simple words: *"Train up a child in the way he should go; and, when he is old, he will not depart from it."* . . . But this experiment has never yet been tried. Education has never yet been brought to bear with one-hundredth part of its potential force upon the natures of children, and, through them, upon the character of men and of the race. . . . Here, then, is a new agency, whose powers are but just beginning to be understood, and whose mighty energies hitherto have been but feebly invoked. . . .

Religious Education

But it will be said that this grand result in practical morals is a consummation of blessedness that can never be attained without religion, and that no community will ever be religious without a religious education. Both these propositions I regard as eternal and immutable truths. . . . That our public schools are not theological seminaries, is admitted. . . . They are debarred by law from inculcating the peculiar and distinctive doctrines of any one religious denomination amongst us. . . . But our system earnestly inculcates all Christian morals; it founds its morals on the basis of religion; it welcomes the religion of the Bible.[3] . . .

I hold it . . . to be one of the excellences, one of the moral beauties, of the Massachusetts system, that there is one place in the land where the children of all the different denominations are brought together for instruction, where the Bible is allowed to speak for itself; one place where the children can kneel at a common

---

[3]Religious instruction in the public schools generated controversy in several northeastern states before the Civil War. It may, as Mann states, have been non-sectarian, but it was emphatically Protestant. Their vociferous objection to it was a factor propelling the growing Catholic minority of the nation into the Democratic Party.

altar, and feel that they have a common Father, and where the services of religion tend to create brothers, and not Ishmaelites. . . .

Such, then, . . . is the Massachusetts system of common schools. Reverently it recognizes and affirms the sovereign rights of the Creator, sedulously and sacredly it guards the religious rights of the creature. . . . In a social and political sense, it is a *free* school-system. It knows no distinction of rich and poor, of bond and free, or between those, who, in the imperfect light of this world, are seeking, through different avenues, to reach the gate of heaven. Without money and without price, it throws open its doors, and spreads the table of its bounty, for all the children of the State. Like the sun, it shines not only upon the good, but upon the evil, that they may become good; and, like the rain, its blessings descend not only upon the just, but upon the unjust, that their injustice may depart from them, and be known no more.

❀ ❀ ❀

The educational improvements advocated by Horace Mann, Henry Bernard, Calvin Stowe, and other school reformers were generally adopted in the Northeast and the Midwest in the years before the Civil War. They were less successful in the South. But despite their obviously superior ability to meet the needs of an industrial society, the new school systems faced opposition even in the North. Rural communities were predictably reluctant to vote themselves higher taxes. Every school reformer found himself wishing, like Thaddeus Stevens in Pennsylvania, that the citizens of his state would "learn to dread ignorance more than taxation." The reforms also threatened deeply cherished traditions of local independence.

In fact the school question was highly indicative of the cultural and moral division in American politics after 1830 between Whigs and Democrats. A recent student of school reform has declared that the best predictor of a person's vote on an educational issue was his party membership. Both Whigs and Democrats favored free public education. But Whigs, in this as in other matters, were more ready to use the power of the state to promote the economic, cultural, and moral improvement of society. "The improvability of our race is without limit," cried New York Governor William Seward in 1840, as he introduced landmark school legislation in his state. Democrats on the other hand, consistent with their Jeffersonian traditions, were deeply suspicious of modern bureaucratic controls and committed to the values of individual independence and local autonomy. A generation earlier in 1817, Thomas Jefferson himself, despite his efforts over many years to persuade his native Virginia to support free public education, opposed a bill that would have achieved that result because it specified state funding and a state board of education which Jefferson regarded as too centralist.

Thus, in the South between 1830 and 1860, colonial educational practices generally persisted, and the advent of free public education was postponed until after the Civil War. In most southern states, between 15 and 20 percent of the adult *white* population remained illiterate. Moreover, beginning in 1830 southern states enacted yet another kind of legislation. Fearful of slave revolts and of the incendiary effects of abolitionist propaganda, they prohibited teaching slaves to read. Consequently, whereas in Massachusetts there was virtually no adult illiteracy in 1860, almost half of the adult southerners, white and black, were unable to read or write.

PART 5

❖ ❖ ❖

Sectionalism and Civil War

1831–1862

1

William Lloyd Garrison

❖ ❖ ❖

The Liberator

1831

*I*n 1839 the New England abolitionist
Theodore Weld and his wife Angelina Grimké published *American Slavery
As It Is: Testimony of a Thousand Witnesses*. In two hundred closely printed
pages drawn from a mountain of evidence from 20,000 southern
newspapers, it described in horrifying detail the physical brutality inflicted
on southern slaves, holding up to public view mutilated bodies, crushed
bones, and flayed backs. Within a year their sensational book had sold
100,000 copies.

It is interesting to reflect that had the book appeared two hundred
years earlier, when Weld's Puritan ancestors first arrived in Boston, it
would scarcely have raised an eyebrow; the Puritans themselves were busily
flogging and branding miscreants, and, in exasperating cases, amputating
their ears or cutting out their tongues. By the beginning of the nineteenth
century, however, not only had corporal punishment disappeared in the
northern states, but the ideal of individual freedom (which Puritans
abominated) had taken such deep root that the age-old practices of bond
servitude and human slavery, normal parts of everyday life in colonial
times, now seemed evil relics of a dark and barbarous past. Massachusetts
was one of the first states to abolish slavery, in 1780. By the 1830s practices
which had once been universal in America were found only in the South,
and Boston was becoming a hotbed of radical abolitionism.

The abolitionists did not invent anti-slavery in the United States; they

THE LIBERATOR   From *The Liberator*, I, (1), January 1, 1831; I (3), January 15,
1831.

transformed it. Cautiously moderate anti-slavery views were widespread after the Revolution, and there were many charitable organizations which worked to encourage the manumission of slaves and to improve the condition of freedmen, often by efforts to colonize them overseas. The most important of these was the American Colonization Society founded in 1816. It enjoyed the patronage of presidents Madison and Monroe, and the support of leading Whigs, including Daniel Webster and Henry Clay who was elected president of the Society in 1836. Many state legislatures, North and South, endorsed the work of the Society, and the federal government provided indirect financial support for the Society's colony of Liberia on the west coast of Africa. Here 16,000 black Americans were resettled before the Civil War.

This moderate and gradual approach to the slavery question was rudely rejected in 1831 by William Lloyd Garrison, a penniless young typesetter, who used scrap type and a rented Boston press to produce the first issue of *The Liberator*. Garrison and his initially small following were not moderates—they scorned compromise. They called themselves "immediatists." Instead of hoping for the gradual disappearance of slavery, they demanded immediate intervention to abolish it everywhere at once. They fiercely attacked the Colonization Society, calling it a cruel and hypocritical perversion of anti-slavery. The great furor which the abolitionists stirred up after 1830 was not between the North and South, for they had no audience in the South. It was a struggle over the character of anti-slavery—a contest for the minds and hearts of northerners.

To the Public

❀ In the month of August, I issued proposals for publishing *The Liberator* in Washington city; but the enterprise, though hailed in different sections of the country, was palsied by public indifference. Since that time, the removal of the *Genuis of Universal Emancipation*[1] to the Seat of Government has rendered less imperious the establishment of a similar periodical in that quarter.

During my recent tour for the purpose of exciting the minds

---

[1] An anti-slavery newspaper edited (1821–1835) by Benjamin Lundy, the pioneer Quaker abolitionist. Garrison had gone south with Lundy in 1829 to assist him and had spent two months in a Baltimore jail for his efforts.

of the people by a series of discourses on the subject of slavery, every place that I visited gave fresh evidence of the fact, that a greater revolution in public sentiment was to be effected in the free states—*and particularly in New-England*—than at the south. I found contempt more bitter, opposition more active, detraction more relentless, prejudice more stubborn, and apathy more frozen, than among the slave owners themselves. Of course, there were individual exceptions to the contrary. This state of things afflicted, but did not dishearten me. I determined, at every hazard, to lift up the standard of emancipation in the eyes of the nation, *within sight of Bunker Hill and in the birth place of liberty.* That standard is now unfurled; and long may it float, unhurt by the spoliations of time or the missiles of a desperate foe—yea, till every chain be broken, and every bondman set free! Let southern oppressors tremble—let their secret abettors tremble—let their northern apologists tremble—let all the enemies of the persecuted blacks tremble.

I deem the publication of my original Prospectus unnecessary, as it has obtained a wide circulation. The principles therein inculcated will be steadily pursued in this paper, excepting that I shall not array myself as the political partisan of any man. In defending the great cause of human rights, I wish to derive the assistance of all religions and of all parties.

Assenting to the "self-evident truth" maintained in the American Declaration of Independence, "that all men are created equal, and endowed by their Creator with certain inalienable rights— among which are life, liberty and the pursuit of happiness," I shall strenuously contend for the immediate enfranchisement of our slave population. In Park-street Church, on the Fourth of July, 1829, in an address on slavery, I unreflectingly assented to the popular but pernicious doctrine of *gradual* abolition. I seize this opportunity to make a full and unequivocal recantation, and thus publicly to ask pardon of my God, of my country, and of my brethren the poor slaves, for having uttered a sentiment so full of timidity, injustice and absurdity. A similar recantation, from my pen, was published in the *Genius of Universal Emancipation* at Baltimore, in September, 1829. My conscience is now satisfied.

I am aware that many object to the severity of my language; but is there not cause for severity? I *will be* as harsh as truth, and as uncompromising as justice. On this subject, I do not wish to think, or speak, or write, with moderation. No! no! Tell a man whose house is on fire, to give a moderate alarm; tell him to moderately rescue his wife from the hands of the ravisher; tell the mother to gradually extricate her babe from the fire into which it has fallen;—but urge me not to use moderation in a cause like the present. I am in earnest—I will not equivocate—I will not excuse—I will not retreat a single inch—AND I WILL BE HEARD. The apathy of the people is enough to make every statue leap from its pedestal, and to hasten the resurrection of the dead.

It is pretended, that I am retarding the cause of emancipation, by the coarseness of my invective, and the precipitancy of my measures. *The charge is not true.* On this question my influence,—humble as it is,—is felt at this moment to a considerable extent, and shall be felt in coming years—not perniciously, but beneficially—not as a curse, but as a blessing; and posterity will bear testimony that I was right. I desire to thank God, that he enables me to disregard "the fear of man which bringeth a snare," and to speak his truth in its simplicity and power.

And here I close with this fresh dedication:

> "Oppression! I have seen thee, face to face,
> And met thy cruel eye and cloudy brow;
> But thy soul-withering glance I fear not now—
> For dread to prouder feelings doth give place
> Of deep abhorrence! Scorning the disgrace
> Of slavish knees that at thy footstool bow,
> I also kneel—but with far other bow
> Do hail thee and thy herd of hirelings base:—
> I swear, while life-blood warms my throbbing veins,
> Still to oppose and thwart, with heart and hand,
> Thy brutalizing sway—'till Afric's chains
> Are burst, and Freedom rules the rescued land,—
> Trampling Oppression and his iron rod:
> *Such is the vow I take*—SO HELP ME GOD!"

District of Columbia

What do many of the professed enemies of slavery mean, by heaping all their reproaches upon the South, and asserting that the crime of oppression is not national? What power but Congress . . . has jurisdiction over the District of Columbia? That District is rotten with the plague, and stinks in the nostrils of the world. Though it is the Seat of our National Government, . . . yet a fouler spot scarcely exists on earth. In it the worst features of slavery are exhibited; and as a mart for slave-traders, it is unequalled. These facts are well known, . . . but who calls for redress? . . .

It is certainly time that a vigorous and systematic effort should be made, from one end of the country to the other, to pull down that natural monument of oppression which towers up in the District. . . . The following petition is now circulating in this city, and has obtained several valuable signatures. A copy may be found at the bookstore of Lincoln & Edmands, No. 59 Washington St., for a few days longer, where all the friends of the cause are earnestly invited to go and subscribe.[2] . . .

To the Free People of Color of the United States

I address you as men—I address you as freemen—I address you as countrymen. You are the rational creatures of one common Creator; you derive from nature the inalienable right of liberty; you are Americans by birth, and entitled to all the benefits of a republican government.

It is true, that no tyrannical masters domineer over your persons; that your bodies are not mutilated by the lash of a driver; that your children are under your own authority, and are not liable to be sold at public or private auction; that you may worship God according to the dictates of your own conscience, and enjoy the fruits of your own labor. But still you remain under many unjust and grievous disabilities; you do not hold that rank in society, which, as free citizens, you ought to occupy; you are looked upon as an inferior caste, hardly superior in your attainments and circumstances to the slaves; you are not sufficiently protected in your persons and rights. This state of things is owing partly to yourselves, but more especially to the prejudices of [the] community. . . .

The question, therefore, should be quickly settled, whether free colored persons, born or naturalized in this country, are not American citizens, and justly entitled to all the rights, privileges and

---

[2]Congress finally abolished the slave trade, although not slavery itself, in the District of Columbia as part of the Compromise of 1850.

immunities of citizens of the several states; and whether the Constitution of the United States makes or authorizes any invidious distinction with regard to the color or condition of free inhabitants.

For myself, I have not the shadow of a doubt on the subject. I believe that the rights of the free colored persons need only to be vindicated before the U.S. Supreme Court, to be obtained; that no prejudice or sophistry, . . . can prevent their acknowledgement; . . . and that the present laws, affecting your condition, are clearly unconstitutional.[3] The fact, that you have been treated, by common consent and common usage, as aliens and brutes, is not proof that such treatment is legal, but only shows the strength, the bitterness, and the blindness of prejudice.

I shall not dwell, at present, upon the subject of colonization, as doubtless the greater portion of you know my views in relation to it, and I believe they fully coincide with yours. . . . As a body, you will inevitably remain in the United States as long as the whites. Consequently, you must strive to get a full and immediate recognition of your rights. Cases of oppression of some of your number are constantly occurring; . . . these are actionable, and must be carried to the Supreme Court for trial. For this purpose, a small fund will be necessary to fee your lawyers.

❂ ❂ ❂

More was at stake in the issue of immediatism versus gradualism than a question of timing. The implicit assumption behind the colonization movement was that the supposed racial inferiority of blacks prohibited their equal assimilation into American society as free persons. Therefore, moderates believed, the abolition of slavery must be gradual in order to permit the resettlement of freedmen overseas. It was for this reason that abolitionists condemned gradualism, calling it a mask behind which there lurked, in Garrison's words, "the monster" of racial prejudice. "The removal of this prejudice is not a matter of opinion," wrote Lydia Maria Child in 1833, "it is a matter of duty. . . . There will, in all human probability, never be any decrease in the black population of the United States. Here they are and here they must remain in very large numbers, do what we will. We may *at once* agree to live together in mutual goodwill." Here was at least one important meaning of immediatism.

---

[3]When Garrison wrote in 1831, the old Federalist John Marshall was still Chief Justice, a fact which may help account for Garrison's optimism. Unfortunately the constitutional issue he raised was not heard by the Supreme Court until 1857, when it was decided by a former Jacksonian politico, Roger B. Taney. In the case of *Dred Scott* v. *Sandford*, Taney ruled that free Negroes were not citizens of the United States.

Their concern to assert the possibility of an equitably biracial society, caused abolitionists also to work to eradicate legal inequalities suffered by free blacks in the North. Under their prodding, blacks in Massachusetts were able to advance more rapidly toward equal rights than in any other state. During the 1840s the Massachusetts law prohibiting interracial marriage was repealed, and public railway facilities were desegregated. Blacks were guaranteed the right to vote on an equal basis with whites and were sometimes elected to local offices. Most Massachusetts public schools were desegregated during the 1840s, and blacks won admission to the state's colleges. In 1848 Harvard's President Everett pledged that any Negro applicant would be judged solely by his qualifying examination, "and if the white students choose to withdraw, all the income of the college will be devoted to his education." In 1855 Boston became the first large city in the nation to integrate its public schools. By the eve of the Civil War, blacks in Massachusetts were no longer, at least politically or legally, second-class citizens.

2

John C. Calhoun and Daniel Webster

❀ ❀ ❀

Speeches on the Compromise Bill
1850

*O*nly a small minority of white northerners were abolitionists. A majority were content with the fact that slavery should continue to exist in the southern states. Indeed, politically, there was little alternative. The individual states alone possessed the power to decide the fate of slavery within their boundaries. Because half the states in 1850 were slave states, nationwide abolition by Constitutional amendment was out of the question.

By 1850, however, a growing number of northerners had resolved that slavery must not be permitted in the western territories which were owned jointly by all American citizens and administered by majority vote in Congress. This was not necessarily a moral stand. Most northern Whigs and many northern Democrats believed, simply, that the West should be reserved for the small, independent, family farmers who, as Jefferson had said, were the "bone and sinew" of the republic.

Before the Mexican War, the territorial question was moot. The Missouri Compromise of 1820 prohibited slavery in all territories north of 36 degrees 30 minutes north latitude, the southern boundary of Missouri. With the single exception of Indian Territory (Oklahoma), all the territories below that line (where slavery was acceptable under the Missouri agreement) had been admitted as states. Then, the victory over Mexico

SPEECHES ON THE COMPROMISE BILL   From *Congressional Globe*, Thirty-first Congress, First session, pp. 452–76.

extended American dominion to the Pacific Ocean. Almost immediately, gold was discovered in California and the suddenly populous province applied for statehood with a constitution prohibiting slavery. This put to risk the balance between free states and slave states in the Senate. This balance, as John C. Calhoun's address of March 4, 1850, indicates, had come to be looked upon by southerners as a guarantee of their power to veto anti-slavery legislation. California must not be admitted as a state without assurances that some of the Mexican acquisition be reserved for new slave states.

Calhoun's speech was delivered in opposition to a compromise bill introduced in the Senate by the "Great Compromiser," Henry Clay. Clay's "Omnibus Bill" included concessions to both North and South in return for concessions on their parts. California would be admitted as a free state but New Mexico Territory (present-day Arizona and New Mexico) would be organized without any reference to slavery. The implication was that New Mexico might later enter the Union as a slave state. Buying and selling slaves (but not slavery itself) would be abolished in the District of Columbia, a concession to anti-slavery northerners. A stronger Fugitive Slave Law, under which runaway slaves who made it to free states would be returned to their masters, was a significant concession to slaveowners.

Not so eloquent as in his youth, Clay was able to deliver only the wannest plea for a spirit of compromise. Far more striking was Calhoun's pro-slavery extremism and the speech of a young anti-slavery senator from New York, William E. Seward. He denounced the Omnibus Bill because of the Fugitive Slave Act, because it did not prohibit slavery in New Mexico, and because it did not abolish slavery in the District of Columbia. In other words, Seward and other abolitionists opposed the Omnibus Bill precisely because it was a compromise. "I AM OPPOSED TO ANY SUCH COMPROMISE," Seward said. "All such legislative compromises [are] radically wrong and essentially vicious." On March 7, a man identified as firmly with Massachusetts as Calhoun was with South Carolina, Seward with anti-slavery, and Clay with compromise, spoke his piece. To the surprise of some, Daniel Webster called on northerners to support Clay's bill.

John C. Calhoun
March 4, 1850

A single section, governed by the will of the numerical majority, has now, in fact, the control of the Government and the entire powers of the system. What was once a constitutional Federal Republic is now converted, in reality, into one as absolute as that of the Autocrat of Russia,[1] and as despotic in its tendency as any absolute Government that ever existed.

As, then, the North has the absolute control over the Government, it is manifest that on all questions between it and the South, where there is diversity of interests, the interests of the latter will be sacrificed to the former, however oppressive the effects may be, as the South possesses no means by which it can resist through the action of the Government. . . .

How can the Union be saved? There is but one way by which it can with any certainty; and that is, by a full and final settlement, on the principle of justice, of the questions at issue between the two sections. The South asks for justice, simple justice, and less she ought not to take. She has no compromise to offer but the Constitution, and no concession or surrender to make. She has already surrendered so much that she has little left to surrender. Such a settlement would go to the root of the evil, and remove all cause of discontent, by satisfying the South she could remain honorably and safely in the Union, and thereby restore the harmony and fraternal feelings between the sections which existed anterior to the Missouri agitation. Nothing else can, with any certainty, finally and forever settle the question at issue, terminate agitation, and save the Union.

But can this be done? Yes, easily; not by the weaker party, for it can of itself do nothing—not even protect itself—but by the stronger. The North has only to will it to accomplish it—to do justice by conceding to the South an equal right in the acquired territory, and to do her duty by causing the stipulations relative to fugitive slaves to be faithfully fulfilled—to cease the agitation of the slave question, and to provide for the insertion of a provision in the Constitution, by an amendment, which will restore the South in substance the power she possessed of protecting herself, before the equilibrium between the sections was destroyed by the action of this Government. There will be no difficulty in devising such a provision—one that will protect the South and which at the same time will improve and strengthen the Government, instead of impairing and weakening it.

But will the North agree to do this? It is for her to answer this question. But, I will say, she cannot refuse, if she has half the love of the Union which she professes to have, or without justly exposing herself to the charge that her love of power and aggrandizement is far greater than her love of the Union. At all events, the responsibility of saving the Union rests on the North, and not the South. . . .

---

[1]To Americans of the nineteenth century, the Czar of Russia was the symbol of reactionary, absolute, repressive government, which in fact the czars were.

Daniel Webster
March 7, 1850

Mr. President, I wish to speak to-day, not as a Massachusetts man, nor as a northern man, but as an American, and a member of the Senate of the United States. . . . It is not to be denied that we live in the midst of strong agitations, and are surrounded by very considerable dangers to our institutions of government. The imprisoned winds are let loose. The East, the West, the North, and the stormy South, all combine to throw the whole ocean into commotion, to toss its billows to the skies, and to disclose its profoundest depths. I do not affect to regard myself, Mr. President, as holding, or as fit to hold, the helm in this combat of the political elements; but I have a duty to perform, and I mean to perform it with fidelity. . . . I speak today for the preservation of the Union. "Hear me for my cause." I speak to-day out of a solicitous and anxious heart, for the restoration to the country of that quiet and that harmony which make the blessings of this Union so rich and so dear to us all. . . .

There has been found at the North, among individuals and among legislators, a disinclination to perform fully their constitutional duties in regard to the return of persons bound to service who have escaped into the free States. In that respect, the South, in my judgment, is right, and the North is wrong. Every member of every Northern legislature is bound by oath, like every other officer in the country, to support the Constitution of the United States; and the article of the Constitution which says to these States that they shall deliver up fugitives from service is as binding in honor and conscience as any other article. . . .

I desire to call to the attention of all sober-minded men at the North, of all conscientious men, of all men who are not carried away by some fanatical idea or some false impression, to their constitutional obligations. I put it to all the sober and sound minds at the North as a question of morals and a question of conscience. What right have they, in their legislative capacity or any other capacity, to endeavor to get round this Constitution, or to embarrass the free exercise of the rights secured by the Constitution to the persons whose slaves escape from them? None at all; none at all. Neither in the forum of conscience, nor before the face of the Constitution, are they, in my opinion, justified in such an attempt. . . .

Now, as to California and New Mexico, I hold slavery to be excluded from those territories by a law even superior to that which admits and sanctions it in Texas—I mean the law of nature—of physical geography—the law of the formation of the earth.[2] That law settles forever, with a strength beyond all terms of human enactment, that slavery cannot exist in California or New Mexico. . . . I look upon it, therefore, as a fixed fact, to use an expression current at this day, that both California and New Mexico are destined to be free, so far as they are settled at all, which I believe, especially in regard to New Mexico, will be very little for a great length of time— free by the arrangement of things by the Power above us. . . . I will say further, that if a resolution, or a law, were now before us, to provide a territorial government for New Mexico, I would not vote to put any prohibition into it whatever. The use of such a prohibition would be idle, as it respects any effect it would have upon the territory; and I would not take pains to reaffirm an ordinance of nature, nor to reenact the will of God. . . . I would put into it no evidence of the votes of superior power, to wound the pride, even whether a just pride, a rational pride, or an irrational pride—to wound the pride of the gentlemen who belong to the Southern states. I have no such object—no such purpose. They would think it a taunt—an indignity. They would think it to be an act of taking away from them what they regard as a proper equality of privilege; and whether they expect to realize any benefit from it or not, they would think it a theoretic wrong—that something more or less derogatory to their character and their rights had taken place. I propose to inflict no such wound upon any body, unless something essentially important to the country, and efficient to the preservation of liberty and freedom, is to be effected. . . .

And now, Mr. President, instead of speaking of the possibility or utility of secession, instead of dwelling in these caverns of darkness, instead of groping with those ideas so full of all that is horrid and horrible, let us come out into the light of day; let us enjoy the fresh air of liberty and union; let us cherish those hopes which belong to us; let us devote ourselves to those great objects that are fit for our consideration and our action; let us raise our conceptions to the magnitude and the importance of the duties that devolve upon us; let our comprehension be as broad as the country for which we act, our aspirations as high as its certain destiny; let us not be pigmies in a case that calls for men. Never did there devolve, on any generation of men, higher trusts than now devolve upon us for the preservation of this Constitution, and the harmony and peace of all who are destined to live under it.

---

[2]Like other northern moderates on the slavery issue (and some southerners), Webster believed that slavery could survive only in environments that supported the plantation system. Proslavery spokesmen like Calhoun, of course, did not agree.

❀ ❀ ❀

The incompatible extremisms of Seward and Calhoun were too much for Henry Clay. His Omnibus Bill failed and he left Washington an exhausted, broken man. He died, as did Webster, in 1853. Ailing from throat cancer so bad that his March 4 speech had to be read for him, Calhoun died on March 30, 1850, croaking sadly, "The South, the poor South!"

Only after his funeral was Stephen A. Douglas of Illinois able to push most of the provisions of Clay's compromise through Congress. With moderates of both the North and South, Douglas played on the very real fears of civil war that the acrimonious debate had aroused. However, Douglas was able to succeed only by splitting the Omnibus Bill into six separate bills. Those which appealed to anti-slavery congressmen were passed with almost entirely northern majorities. Those which were concessions to pro-slavery congressmen were passed with largely southern majorities. Only four out of sixty senators voted for all of Douglas's bills, only eleven for five of the six. The Compromise of 1850 was not a compromise at all. It was a delaying action.

The sentiments expressed in 1850 by Seward, Calhoun, and Webster continued to reverberate in Congress and the country as the sectional crisis continued. Strident attacks on slavery, like Seward's became more common and won more approbation in the North. They increasingly reflected a shrill anti-southernism that seemed to confirm Calhoun's nightmare of an ever more powerful North threatening the institutions of the South. Seward himself came to speak of an "irrepressible conflict" between the two sections and even the more moderate Abraham Lincoln said that a house divided could not stand: the United States would have to become all slave or all free. When Lincoln was elected to the presidency in 1860, Calhoun's own South Carolina led the parade of southern states out of the Union and into the great rebellion.

In 1850 Webster was disgraced in the eyes of some New Englanders for his willingness to compromise with an institution that they, like William Seward, saw as unambivalently evil. Nevertheless, in his exaltation of the Union as the basis of the precious liberties of the American people, Webster gave voice to the lone principle that was to sustain the United States government during the first two and a half years of the great Civil War—Union and Liberty were one and inseparable.

3

Abraham Lincoln
❂ ❂ ❂

A House Divided
1858

*F*or Americans in the 1850s a purely
moral judgment on the question of slavery was easily reached, for or
against, depending on the part of the country from which they came.
Translating that moral position into national policy was much more
difficult. Under the Constitution slavery was a "domestic institution," left
to the government of the individual states. Anti-slavery northerners,
therefore, had no opportunity to cast their ballots in any constituency
which actually possessed jurisdiction over the nation's four million slaves.
The British had been able to abolish slavery by act of Parliament, despite
the opposition of West Indian planters. No act of Congress, however, could
free the southern slaves. In effect the Constitution made slavery legally
untouchable in the United States, even though there were only about
400,000 slaveowners in a population of 30 million.

Federal policy could affect slavery only in a few, peripheral areas.
The most important of these were the territories—frontier parts of the
nation which had not yet been admitted to statehood but were governed by
Congress itself. Here the slavery debate came to a focus in the 1850s, not
because there were many slaves in the territories (there were hardly any),
but because the territorial issue was the only forum in which a *national*
policy on slavery could be addressed. For both sides, then, the territorial
question was a symbolic one. This fact did not make it any less important.
In a democratic nation loyalty, and a willingness to respect the decisions

A HOUSE DIVIDED   Speech at Chicago, Illinois, July 10, 1858. From *The Illinois Political
Campaign of 1858*, Library of Congress (Washington: U.S. Government Printing Office, 1958), pp. 41–47.

of the majority, depends on the extent to which citizens see in the nation a reflection of their own basic values.

Prior to 1850, Congress had compromised between the two sections of the nation by excluding slavery from the northern half of the territories while permitting it to expand into the southern half. In 1787 Congress had drawn the line along the Ohio River, and in the Missouri Compromise of 1820, it extended the line across the territories to the Rocky Mountains. However, in 1850 when it came time to decide the status of slavery in the new territories acquired from Mexico, both sides sharply raised their demands. "Free-Soil" northerners now insisted that slavery be prohibited in *all* the new territories, and southerners claimed that since the territories belonged to the whole nation, Congress had no right to exclude the South from any of them.

Congress attempted to find a new way out of its difficulties in 1850 when it adopted the doctrine of "Popular Sovereignty." According to this plan, Congress would not decide the question in advance, but would leave it open to be decided locally by the settlers in the new territories themselves. Subsequent events, however, proved that this apparently democratic solution to the problem, enacted in the Compromise of 1850, was a grave mistake. A good compromise should provide each side with half a loaf, but Popular Sovereignty satisfied only the desire for compromise itself, while failing to contribute anything to the real interests of either of the opposing sections. Angry northerners denounced it as a retreat from the earlier willingness of Congress to condemn slavery by excluding it from at least part of the territories. And thoughtful southerners realized that few slaveowners would risk settling in a territory which might before long vote to abolish the institution.

The error was compounded in 1854 when Senator Stephen Douglas of Illinois, who had guided the Compromise of 1850 through Congress, yielded to southern pressures and introduced Popular Sovereignty into Kansas. Douglas was trying to organize a territorial government in a region from which slavery had been excluded by the Missouri Compromise of 1820. Reluctantly, he included in the Kansas–Nebraska Act a provision repealing the Missouri Compromise line. "It will raise a hell of a storm," he said.

It was the understatement of the century. The storm raised by the Kansas–Nebraska Act did not subside until Lee surrendered to Grant in 1865. In droves outraged northerners deserted both of the major political parties in 1854 to join a new party committed to free-soil principles: the Republican Party. Because the national parties had helped to hold the country together, their collapse was a major event in the gradual descent into civil war. The new Republican Party was not national; it was strictly a sectional party. Therefore it aggravated the division instead of promoting unity.

Abraham Lincoln, a former Whig who helped to organize the Republican Party in Illinois, won, in 1858, its nomination to the Senate seat held by Stephen Douglas. In the famous series of campaign debates which followed, Douglas the Democrat defended Popular Sovereignty in the territories, while Lincoln the Republican advocated Congressional prohibition. "A house divided against itself cannot stand," Lincoln told the party convention which nominated him, and he repeated the assertion verbatim in this address delivered a few days later in Chicago.

❀ Judge Douglas made two points upon my recent speech at Springfield. He says they are to be the issues of this campaign. The first one of these points he bases upon the language . . . which I believe I can quote correctly from memory. I said there that,

> A house divided against itself cannot stand. I believe this government cannot endure permanently half slave and half free. I do not expect the Union to be dissolved, I do not expect the house to fall, but I do expect it will cease to be divided. It will become all one thing or the other. Either the opponents of slavery will arrest the spread of it, and place it where the public mind shall rest in the belief that it is in the course of ultimate extinction, or its advocates will push it forward until it shall become alike lawful in all the States, North as well as South.

In this paragraph which I have quoted in your hearing, . . . Judge Douglas thinks he discovers great political heresy. . . . He says I am in favor of making all the States of this Union uniform in all their internal regulations; that in all their domestic concerns I am in favor of making them entirely uniform. . . . He says that I am in favor of making war by the North upon the South for the extinction of slavery. . . . Now, it is singular enough, if you will carefully read that passage over, that I did not say that I was in favor of anything in it. I only said what I expected would take place. I made a prediction only—it may have been a foolish one perhaps. I did not even say that I desired that slavery should be put in course of ultimate extinction. I do say so now, however, [Great applause] so there need be no longer any difficulty about that. [Applause] . . .

Gentlemen, Judge Douglas informed you that this speech of mine was probably carefully prepared. I admit that it was. I am not master of language; I have not a fine education; . . . but I do not believe the language I employed bears any such construction as

Judge Douglas put upon it. . . . I know what I meant, and I will not leave this crowd in doubt, if I can explain it to them. . . .

I am not, in the first place, unaware that this Government has endured eighty-two years, half slave and half free. I know that. I am tolerably well acquainted with the history of the country. . . . I *believe*—and that is what I meant to allude to there—I *believe* it has endured because, during all that time, until the introduction of the Nebraska Bill, the public mind did rest, all the time, in the belief that slavery was in course of ultimate extinction. ["Good!" "Good!" and applause] . . . I have always hated slavery, I think as much as any Abolitionist. [Applause] I have been an Old Line Whig. I have always hated it, but I have always been quiet about it until this new era of the introduction of the Nebraska Bill began. I always believed that everybody was against it, and that it was in course of ultimate extinction. . . .

I have said a hundred times, and I have now no inclination to take it back, that I believe there is no right, and ought to be no inclination in the people of the free States to enter into the slave States, and interfere with the question of slavery at all. I have said that always. Judge Douglas has heard me say it. . . . I think that I have said it in your hearing, . . . that each community, as a State, has a right to do exactly as it pleases with all the concerns within that State that interfere with the rights of no other State, and that the general government, upon principle, has no right to interfere with anything other than that general class of things that does concern the whole. . . . I have said, as illustrations, that I do not believe in the right of Illinois to interfere with the cranberry laws of Indiana, the oyster laws of Virginia, or the liquor laws of Maine. I have said these things over and over again. . . .

How is it, then, that Judge Douglas infers, because I hope to see slavery put where the public mind shall rest in the belief that it is in the course of ultimate extinction, that I am in favor of Illinois going over and interfering with the cranberry laws of Indiana? What can authorize him to draw any such inference? I suppose there might be one thing that at least enabled *him* to draw such an inference, . . . that is, because he looks upon all this matter of slavery as an exceedingly little thing—this matter of keeping one-sixth of the population of the whole nation in a state of oppression and tyranny unequalled in the world. He looks upon it as being an exceedingly little thing—only equal to the question of the cranberry laws of Indiana—as something having no moral question in it. . . . Now it so happens . . . that the Judge thinks thus; and it so happens that there is a vast portion of the American people that do *not* look upon that matter as being this very little thing. They look upon it as a vast moral evil; they can prove it is such by the writings of those who gave us the blessings of liberty which we enjoy. [Great applause] . . .

We were often . . . in the course of Judge Douglas' speech last night, reminded that this government was made for white men. . . . Well, that is putting it into a shape in which no one wants to deny it, but the Judge then goes into his passion for drawing inferences that are not warranted. I protest, now and forever, against that counterfeit logic which presumes that because I do not want a Negro woman for a slave, I do necessarily want her for a wife. [Laughter and cheers] My understanding is that I need not have her for either, but as God made us separate, we can leave one another alone and do one another much good thereby. . . .

Now, it happens that we meet together once every year, sometime about the 4th of July, for some reason or other. These 4th of July gatherings I suppose have their uses. If you will indulge me, I will state what I suppose to be some of them.

We are now a mighty nation, we are thirty . . . millions of people, and we own and inhabit about one-fifteenth part of the dry land of the whole earth. We run our memory back over the pages of history for about eighty-two years and we discover . . . a race of men living in that day whom we claim as our fathers and grandfathers; they were iron men, they fought for the principle that they were contending for; and we understand that by what they then did it has followed that the degree of prosperity that we now enjoy has come to us. We hold this annual celebration to remind ourselves of all the good done in this process of time, of how it was done and who did it, and how we are historically connected with it; and we go from these meetings in better humor with ourselves—we feel more attached the one to the other, and more firmly bound to the country we inhabit. . . . But after we have done all this we have not yet reached the whole. . . . We have besides these men—descended by blood from our ancestors—among us perhaps half our people who are not descendants at all of these men, they are men who have come from Europe—German, Irish, French and Scandinavian—men that have come from Europe themselves, or whose ancestors have . . . settled here, finding themselves our equals in all things. If they look back through this history to trace their connection with those days by blood, they find they have none. . . . But when they look through that old Declaration of Independence they find that those old men say that "We hold these truths to be self-evident, that all men are created equal," and then they feel that that moral sentiment taught in that day evidences their relation to those men, that it is the father of all moral principle in them, and that they have a right to claim it as though they were blood of the blood, and flesh of the flesh of the men who wrote that Declaration. [Loud and long-continued applause] And so they are. That is the electric cord in that Declaration that links the hearts of patriotic and liberty-loving men together, that will link those patriotic hearts as long as the love of freedom exists in the minds of men throughout the world. [Applause]

Now, sirs, for the purpose of . . . holding that the Declaration of Independence did not mean anything at all, we have Judge Douglas giving his exposition of what the Declaration of Independence means, and we have him saying that [it means] the people of America are equal to the people of England. According to his construction, you Germans[1] are not connected with it. Now I ask you in all soberness, if all these things, . . . if taught to our children, and repeated to them, do not tend to rub out the sentiment of liberty in the country, and to transform this Government into a government of some other form.

Those arguments that are made, that the inferior race are to be treated [only] with as much allowance as they are capable of enjoying. . . . What are these arguments? They are the arguments that kings have made for enslaving the people in all ages of the world. . . . And this argument of the Judge is the same old serpent that says you work and I eat, you toil and I will enjoy the fruits of it. Turn it whatever way you will—whether it come from the mouth of a king [as] an excuse for enslaving the people of his country, or from the mouth of men of one race as a reason for enslaving the men of another race, it is all the same old serpent. . . . I should like to know if taking this old Declaration of Independence, which declares that all men are equal upon principle, and making exceptions to it, where it will stop? If one man says it does not mean a Negro, why may not another say it does not mean some other man? If that Declaration is not the truth, let us get the Statute book in which we find it and tear it out! Who is so bold as to do it! [Cries of "no, no"] . . .

My friend has said to me that I am a poor hand to quote Scripture. I will try it again, however. It is said in one of the admonitions of the Lord, "As your Father in Heaven is perfect, be ye also perfect." The Savior, I suppose, did not expect that any human

---

[1]According to some accounts, a German political club had just pushed its way into the crowd.

creature could be perfect as the Father in Heaven; but . . . he set that up as a standard, and he who did most toward reaching that standard, attained the highest degree of moral perfection. So I say in relation to the principle that all men are created equal, let it be as nearly reached as we can. If we cannot give freedom to every creature, let us do nothing that will impose slavery upon any other creature. [Applause] . . .

My friends, I have detained you about as long as I desired to do, and I have only to say, let us discard all this quibbling about this man and the other man—this race and that race and the other race being inferior, and therefore they must be placed in an inferior position—discarding our standard that we have left us. Let us discard all these things, and unite as one people throughout this land, until we shall once more stand up declaring that all men are created equal. [A torrent of applause and cheers]

❖ ❖ ❖

The Lincoln–Douglas debates made it clear that there were many questions on which the two candidates were not far apart. Douglas no less than Lincoln approved of the fact that slavery was prohibited in their own state. And Lincoln did not object any more than Douglas did to the civil inequalities which were suffered by the free blacks there. "There is," Lincoln said at one point, in a tone very different from that of his Chicago speech, "a physical difference between the white and black races which I believe will forever forbid the two races living together on terms of social and political equality. And inasmuch as they cannot so live, while they do remain together there must be the position of superior and inferior, and I as much as any other man am in favor of having the superior position assigned to the white race." Despite what he had said in Chicago, Lincoln was not an abolitionist. He was an anti-slavery moderate who hoped that the abolition of slavery would occur gradually and who tended to favor the colonization of freedmen overseas.

Nor did Lincoln have any specific plan to abolish slavery even gradually. Speaking of the southerners he said, "I surely will not blame them for not doing what I should not know how to do myself. If all earthly power were given me, I should not know what to do, as to the existing institution." Like Douglas, Lincoln denied that under the Constitution the free states had any right to interfere with slavery in the states where it already existed. The dilemma Lincoln made for himself was not easily resolved, as Douglas was quick to point out. On one hand Lincoln said, "This government cannot endure permanently half slave and half free," and on the other he failed to offer any realistic means of abolishing slavery. "How then," Douglas cogently asked, "does Lincoln propose to save the Union?"

For his part Douglas demanded to know why the nation could not continue to exist half slave and half free. That was the condition in which the Founding Fathers had made it; it had prospered in that condition for eighty years; both of the great national parties, Whigs and Democrats, had formerly respected the division. The only threat to the union which Douglas could see was that posed by the Republican Party—"A party," he charged, "which appeals to northern passion, northern pride, northern ambition and northern prejudices," in order "to array all the Northern States in one body against the South."

Republicans had only one policy to propose—the exclusion of slavery from the territories. Douglas could see neither how this would "save the Union" in Lincoln's sense, nor make any practical difference, since the territories in question were not well suited for slavery anyway. Evidently the issue was important only as a gesture to demonstrate national hostility to slavery, and this Douglas rejected as outside the powers of the federal government. Under the Constitution moral questions were wisely left to the states. "If we will only act conscientiously and rigidly upon this great principle," Douglas said, "which guarantees to each State and Territory the right to do as it pleases on all things local and domestic instead of Congress interfering, we will continue at peace one with another."

As the Chicago speech illustrates, however, it was precisely the moral bonds of the union which were uppermost in Lincoln's mind. In his view a nation indifferent to the moral sentiments of the people could remain neither whole nor free.

4

Alexander Hamilton Stephens

❁ ❁ ❁

Slavery the Cornerstone
1861

Patriotism comes naturally to most people because their nation seems merely a somewhat larger and more glorious version of their home towns. Only Southerners, of all Americans, have ever had to choose between the two. For Alexander H. Stephens, home was a singularly ugly white frame house next to the railroad tracks in Crawfordville, Georgia, which he was pleased to call, rather fancifully, "Liberty Hall." Here, on a few acres of red Georgia clay, beside the graves of the parents who had died in his childhood, Stephens lived out his life a solitary bachelor, practicing law, and venturing abroad only as far as Washington to represent his neighbors in Congress.

Stephens was a strange wraith of a man, whose immature body, piping voice, and feeble health caused him to look, in a friend's words, "as if the man had only a two weeks' purchase on life." Personally he seemed to consist of little more than brain, and even this was afflicted with gloomy forebodings and neurotic suspicions. He commanded a kind of brittle intelligence, which caused him to be esteemed in his section as a scholar-statesman, although to us he appears more the pedant than anything else.

The fixed principles of Alexander Stephens' life were two: the Constitution as it had been interpreted by two generations of southern advocates of states rights, and the "Old Union"—the union created by the Founding Fathers in which slavery had been unquestioned, abolitionist attacks on the South unknown, and the preeminence of southern statesmen a matter of course. From this exalted ground the tiny Georgian

SLAVERY THE CORNERSTONE   Speech at Savannah, Georgia, March 21, 1861. From *The Rebellion Record*, ed. Frank Moore (New York, 1861), I, 44–46.

viewed all more recent developments with disdain, and all his own contemporaries as pygmies.

During the 1840s his conservative Unionism led Stephens into the Whig Party where he bitterly attacked Polk, condemned the Mexican war, and fought for acceptance by Georgia of the Compromise of 1850. When the Whig Party collapsed in the South, he tried to organize a "Constitutional Union" party before he reluctantly came over to the Democratic camp. As pressure for secession mounted in the South he opposed it, not from any satisfaction with the present state of things, but out of conservative fear that an independent South could only make matters worse. "Revolutions are much easier started than controlled," he observed gloomily. "Human passions are like winds; when aroused they sweep everything before them in their fury."

Despite his efforts Georgia seceded, and a few weeks later a reluctant Stephens was elected Confederate vice-president, an indication of how few men of stature there were in the Confederacy to choose from. Stephens was the presiding genius of the Confederate Constitutional Convention—helping to draft a constitution which, except in a few particulars, mimicked the old. He seems to have taken some satisfaction in this work, even proposing to admit non-slave states into the Confederacy. Perhaps the new constitution could become the basis for a restoration of the Old Union after all! During his inauguration he sulked and said little, but a few weeks later, at Savannah, he spoke at length in explication of the new document.

We are in the midst of one of the greatest epochs in our history. The last ninety days will mark one of the most memorable eras in the history of modern civilization. . . . Seven States have, within the last three months, thrown off an old Government and formed a new. This revolution has been signally marked, up to this time, by the fact of its having been accomplished without the loss of a single drop of blood.[1] [Applause] This new Constitution, or form of government, constitutes the subject to which your attention will be partly invited.

In reference to it, I make this first general remark: It amply secures all our ancient rights, franchises, and privileges. . . . All the

---

[1] The fighting began at Ft. Sumter three weeks later.

essentials of the old Constitution, which have endeared it to the hearts of the American people, have been preserved and perpetuated. [Applause] Some changes have been made. . . . They form great improvements upon the old Constitution. So, taking the whole new Constitution, I have no hesitancy in giving it as my judgment, that it is decidedly better than the old. [Applause] Allow me briefly to allude to some of these improvements. . . .

We allow the imposition of no duty with a view of giving advantage to one class of persons, in any trade or business, over those of another. . . . This old thorn of the tariff,[2] which occasioned the cause of so much irritation in the old body politic, is removed forever from the new. [Applause]

Again, the subject of internal improvements, under the power of Congress to regulate commerce, is put at rest under our system. . . . The true principle is to subject commerce of every locality to whatever burdens may be necessary to facilitate it. If the Charleston harbor needs improvement, let the commerce of Charleston bear the burden. . . . This is again the broad principle of perfect equality and justice. [Applause] And it is specially held forth and established in our new Constitution. . . .

But not to be tedious in enumerating the numerous changes for the better, allow me to allude to one other—though last, not least: the new Constitution has put at rest *forever* all the agitating questions relating to our peculiar institutions—African slavery as it exists among us—the proper *status* of the Negro in our form of civilization. This was the immediate cause of the late rupture and present revolution. Jefferson, in his forecast, had anticipated this, as the "rock upon which the old Union would split." He was right. . . . But whether he full comprehended the great truth upon which that rock stood and stands, may be doubted. The prevailing ideas entertained by him and most of the leading statesmen at the time of the formation of the old Constitution were, that the enslavement of the African was in violation of the laws of nature; that it was wrong in principle, socially, morally, and politically. It was an evil they knew not well how to deal with; but the general opinion of the men of that day was, that, somehow or other, in the order of Providence, the institution would be evanescent and pass away. . . .

Those ideas, however, were fundamentally wrong. They rested upon the assumption of the equality of races. This was an

---

[2]The Confederate Constitution specifically prohibited protective tariffs, as well as any appropriation by the Confederate Congress for internal improvements.

error. It was a sandy foundation, and the idea of a Government built upon it—when the "storm came and the wind blew, it *fell*."

Our new Government is founded upon exactly the opposite ideas; its foundations are laid, its cornerstone rests, upon the great truth that the Negro is not equal to the white man; that slavery, subordination to the superior race, is his natural and moral condition. [Applause] This, our new Government, is the first, in the history of the world, based upon this great physical, philosophical, and moral truth.

This truth has been slow in the progress of its development,[3] like all other truths in the various departments of science. It is so even amongst us. Many who hear me, perhaps, can recollect well that this truth was not generally admitted, even within their day. The errors of the past generation still clung to many as late as twenty years ago. Those at the North who still cling to these errors with a zeal above knowledge, we justly denominate fanatics. All fanaticism springs from an aberration of the mind; from a defect in reasoning. It is a species of insanity. One of the most striking characteristics of insanity, in many instances, is, forming correct conclusions from fancied or erroneous premises; so with the *anti-slavery* fanatics: their conclusions are right if their premises are. They assume that the Negro is equal, and hence conclude that he is entitled to equal privileges and rights, with the white man. If their premises were correct, their conclusions would be logical and just; but their premises being wrong, their whole argument fails. . . .

In the conflict thus far, success has been on our side, complete throughout the length and breadth of the Confederate States. It is upon this, as I have stated, our social fabric is firmly planted; and I cannot permit myself to doubt the ultimate success of a full recognition of this principle throughout the civilized and enlightened world.

As I have stated, the truth of this principle may be slow in development, as all truths are, and ever have been, in the various branches of science. It was so with the principles announced by Galileo. . . . Now they are universally acknowledged. May we not therefore look with confidence to the ultimate universal acknowledgment of the truths upon which our system rests? It is the first Government ever instituted upon principles in strict conformity to nature, and the ordination of Providence, in furnishing the

---

[3]The argument that slavery was not a necessary evil but a positive good had begun to appear in the writings of southern apologists during the 1830s.

materials of human society. Many governments have been founded upon the principles of certain classes; but the classes thus enslaved, were of the same race, and in violation of the laws of nature. Our system commits no such violation of nature's laws. The Negro by nature . . . is fitted for that condition which he occupies in our system.

The architect, in the construction of buildings, lays the foundation with the proper material—the granite—then comes the brick or the marble. The substratum of our society is made of the material fitted by nature for it, and by experience we know that it is the best, not only for the superior but for the inferior race, that it should be so. It is, indeed, in conformity with the Creator. It is not for us to inquire into the wisdom of his ordinances or to question them. For his own purposes he has made one race to differ from another, as he has made "one star to differ from another in glory."

The great objects of humanity are best attained, when conformed to his laws and decrees, in the formation of Governments as well as in all things else. Our Confederacy is founded upon principles in strict conformity with these laws. This stone which was rejected by the first builders "is become the chief stone of the corner" in our new edifice. [Applause]

❖ ❖ ❖

Confederates who genuinely believed in the sacred cause soon had reason to repent having chosen Stephens to help lead it. He was a defeatist from the beginning, describing the Confederate leadership with words like "weak," "imbecile," "selfish," "unscrupulous." His personal dislike of President Jefferson Davis was so intense that during most of the war the two chief officers of the Confederacy were not on speaking terms. The wife of one cabinet officer recalled in her diary that even as the new government travelled by train to Richmond in 1861, Stephens harangued them with prophecies of imminent doom.

Stephens soon departed Richmond, ignoring his constitutional duty to preside over the Senate there, and chose instead to sit the war out in Crawfordville, brooding among the family tombs. Here he encouraged Governor Joseph E. Brown to obstruct the Confederate war effort, disputing with the Davis government the constitutional propriety of such matters as conscription, war finance, and emergency troop supply. What did it matter that the Confederacy foundered for lack of men or supplies to feed them? "Better that Richmond should fall," he wrote, "and that the enemy's armies should sweep over our whole country from Potomac to the Gulf, than that our people should submissively yield obedience to one of these edicts."

It was an indication of the contradictions with which the brief history of the Confederacy is riddled that Stephens' obstructionism did not seriously diminish his popularity in Georgia. After the war he and Brown allied with the forces of the "New South," promoting business expansion and industry instead of the agrarianism of the past. Although his health was now so poor that he was confined to a wheelchair, and he was much of the time stupefied by injections of morphine, he served another five terms in Congress. When he died in 1882, he had just been elected governor of the state.

5

Abraham Lincoln
❊ ❊ ❊

The Emancipation Proclamation
1862

*D*uring the secession crisis of 1861, when border state moderates tried to head off the impending Civil War by a law guaranteeing slavery in some of the western territories, President-elect Abraham Lincoln let it be known that he would accept, indeed sponsor, an amendment to the Constitution "forever guaranteeing" slavery in those states where it already existed. This was not enough for southern secessionists, just as permitting slavery in any of the territories was too much for Lincoln. His Republican party existed because of the determination of the northern majority to prevent slavery from expanding into the West.

During the first two years of the Civil War, Lincoln repeatedly stated that his sole object was simply to preserve the Union. Not only was the president no abolitionist, political and military realities mandated that he not attack slavery as an institution. Only a minority of northerners were abolitionists. Most felt no overwhelming moral objection to the idea of black slavery. Many, Lincoln believed, would not support a war aimed at destroying the institution. Moreover, five slave states remained loyal to the Union. Lincoln had repeatedly assured the leaders of strategically vital Kentucky that he has no designs on the "peculiar institution."

By mid 1862, circumstances had changed. Kentucky and the other

THE EMANCIPATION PROCLAMATION   From *U.S. Statutes at Large*, XII, 1268–69.

loyal slave states were secure. Large parts of the Confederacy had been occupied. And the influence of the abolitionists in Lincoln's Republican party had increased as the casualty lists lengthened and northern bitterness towards southern "slavocrats" increased. Lincoln had also learned the military value of confiscating the human property of the enemy. When Union armies occupied plantations, or were inundated by runaway slaves, the "human contraband" was put to work. The southern economy was thus made so much the weaker and Union military might so much the stronger. On July 22, 1862, Lincoln read to his cabinet a rough draft of a presidential order that would free all slaves in areas still in rebellion against the United States government as of a date still to be determined.

Not only would such a proclamation encourage slaves to flee their Confederate masters, it was remotely possible that the threat of losing their slaves would prompt powerful southerners to force peace on the none too popular government of Jefferson Davis. At the same time, by leaving untouched slavery in territory under Union control, Lincoln's order would neither test the extent of his wartime powers nor unduly frighten the loyal slaveowners of Missouri, Kentucky, Maryland, and those parts of the Confederacy already conquered.

Secretary of State William Seward, once a radical firebrand, now a model of caution, urged Lincoln not to issue the order until Union armies had won a significant military victory. Only after suffering a defeat was the South likely to respond to such a proclamation. Only when Union forces held the initiative would the proclamation appear to be a positive policy rather than an act of desperation.

Lincoln concurred and, on September 17, 1862, won his victory. Attempting to flank Washington D.C., Robert E. Lee had led his army into Maryland. On the attack for the first time, his troops were soundly beaten at the Battle of Antietam. Five days later Lincoln issued the Emancipation Proclamation.

By the President of the United States of America: A Proclamation.

Whereas on the 22d day of September, A.D. 1862, a proclamation was issued by the President of the United States, containing, among other things, the following, to wit:

"That on the 1st day of January, A.D. 1863, all persons held as slaves within any State or designated part of a State the people whereof shall then be in rebellion against the United States shall be then, thenceforward, and forever free; and the executive government of the United States, including the military and naval authority thereof, will recognize and maintain the freedom of such persons and will do no act or acts to repress such persons, or any of them, in any efforts they may make for their actual freedom.

"That the executive will on the 1st day of January aforesaid, by proclamation, designate the States and parts of the States, if any, in which the people thereof, respectively, shall then be in rebellion against the United States; and the fact that any State or the people thereof shall on that day be in good faith represented in the Congress of the United States by members chosen thereto at elections wherein a majority of the qualified voters of such States shall have participated shall, in the absence of strong countervailing testimony, be deemed conclusive evidence that such State and the people thereof are not then in rebellion against the United States."

Now, therefore, I, Abraham Lincoln, President of the United States, by virtue of the power in me vested as Commander-in-Chief of the Army and Navy of the United States in time of actual armed rebellion against the authority and government of the United States, and as a fit and necessary war measure for suppressing said rebellion, do, on this 1st day of January, A.D. 1863, and in accordance with my purpose so to do, publicly proclaimed for the full period of one hundred days from the first day above mentioned, order and designate as the States and parts of States wherein the people thereof, respectively, are this day in rebellion against the United States the following, to wit:

Arkansas, Texas, Louisiana (except the parishes of St. Bernard, Plaquemines, Jefferson, St. John, St. Charles, St. James, Ascension, Assumption, Terrebonne, Lafourche, St. Mary, St. Martin, and Orleans, including the city of New Orleans), Mississippi, Alabama, Florida, Georgia, South Carolina, North Carolina, and Virginia (except the forty-eight counties designated as West Virginia, and also the counties of Berkeley, Accomac, Northhampton, Elizabeth City, York, Princess Anne, and Norfolk, including the cities of Norfolk and Portsmouth), and which excepted parts are for the present left precisely as if this proclamation were not issued.

And by virtue of the power and for the purpose aforesaid, I do order and declare that all persons held as slaves within said designated States and parts of States are, and henceforward shall be free; and that the Executive Government of the United States, including the military and naval authorities thereof, will recognize and maintain the freedom of said persons.

And I hereby enjoin upon the people so declared to be free to abstain from all violence, unless in necessary self-defense; and I recommend to them that, in all cases when allowed, they labor faithfully for reasonable wages.

And I further declare and make known that such persons of suitable condition will be received into the armed service of the United States to garrison forts, positions, stations, and other places, and to man vessels of all sorts in said service.

And upon this act, sincerely believed to be an act of justice, warranted by the Constitution upon military necessity, I invoke the considerate judgment of mankind and the gracious favor of Almighty God.

❖ ❖ ❖

It has often been observed that, on the moment of publication, the Emancipation Proclamation did not free a single slave. This is true. People held in bondage within the Union were explicitly and specifically exempted from emancipation. Over the slaves in rebel-held territory, of course, Lincoln held no actual authority.

The truism is also irrelevant. On January 1, 1863, Lincoln could no more free slaves within the Union, even in the District of Columbia, than could any president before him. Slavery remained a domestic institution of the loyal slave states. Nationally, slavery could be abolished only, as was eventually done, by an amendment to the Constitution. The District of Columbia remained under the authority of Congress.

The implication of the truism that Lincoln's Proclamation struck no blow against slavery is equally without merit. As a military measure which the Commander in Chief might indeed enact, the Emancipation Proclamation meant that each Union advance after January 1, 1863—and it was reasonable to assume that the Union armies would continue to advance—would free hundreds of thousands of slaves. With the peculiar institution thus upended in its heartland, it would only be a matter of time, as Lincoln surely knew, before slavery was abolished.

Others understood this as well. The abolition of slavery became a tacit war aim after 1863. Union troops marched into battle singing *The Battle Hymn of the Republic* and *John Brown's Body*, rousing anti-slavery anthems. Moreover, if Lincoln's order did not panic leading Confederates into seeking peace before January 1, 1863, news of the Proclamation apparently encouraged even more blacks to abandon their masters when they learned there was a Union army nearby. By the end of the war, 150,000 black men had served in Union blue. Hundreds of thousands more worked building fortifications and peforming other non-combat tasks, thereby releasing soldiers for fighting.

APPENDIX

❀ ❀ ❀

The Charter Documents
1776–1971

1

❖ ❖ ❖

The Declaration of Independence
1776

"*B*y every Post and every day," John Adams exulted in the spring of 1776, "Independence rolls in on us like a torrent." During the preceding year British troops sent to the colonies to restore order had met with stubborn resistance—first from local militia, then from the "Army of the United Colonies" under the command of General George Washington. There was fighting in Massachusetts, Canada, and North Carolina. Royal governors, like Lord Dunmore in Virginia, had fled to the relative safety of British warships anchored offshore, where they pretended to exercise authority over colonies which had in fact been self-governing for months.

In May, Virginia, the oldest, richest, and most populous of the colonies, instructed its delegates to the Continental Congress in Philadelphia to vote for independence. Therefore on June 7 Richard Henry Lee introduced in Congress three resolutions calling for independence, a military alliance with France, and a plan for the confederation of the colonies. Congress appointed committees to attend to all three, including a committee to draft a declaration of independence.

It was mostly accidental that Thomas Jefferson became its author. He was probably the least important member of the Virginia delegation.

THE DECLARATION OF INDEPENDENCE   Reprinted from the facsimile of the original, engrossed copy in the National Archives.

Young (age 33), shy, and somewhat awkward in appearance, neither especially rich as a landowner nor prominent as a lawyer, Jefferson had been sent to Congress as an alternate and had scarcely opened his mouth during its sessions. Moreover he was only recently married and greatly preoccupied with his eventual masterpiece, the construction of a Palladian villa on an improbable hilltop site, where his bride still kept house in makeshift tents. Jefferson was absent from Congress for four months that spring, buying wine for his cellar and stocking his park with deer. He only chanced to return from Monticello to Philadelphia in time to be appointed to the committee to prepare the Declaration. Jefferson had one important qualification for the assignment. The other colonies deferred to the Virginians, and among the Virginians, a delegation which included splendid orators, superb horsemen and soldiers, opulent committee managers, there was only one with any patience for paperwork. The task fell to the bookish Jefferson by default.

Nor did it call for much originality. Everybody knew how a "declaration" was supposed to go. In law declarations were filed after bringing an action in court; they listed the grounds for complaint. Similarly, in constitutional practice, declarations were issued to explain actions already taken. It was a form followed by, among others, William of Orange when he seized the British throne in 1688 and by Congress itself in 1775 in its Declaration of the Causes of Taking Up Arms. The prescribed form was a modified version of the petition. It required first a brief statement of the just basis of the rights in question, then a detailed list of "grievances," or violations of those rights, and finally the proposed remedy. This form Jefferson followed exactly, borrowing extensively from other documents produced during the revolutionary controversy, not "aiming at originality of principle or sentiment," he afterwards said, but only "to place before mankind the common sense of the subject."

Thus to Jefferson and his contemporaries the most important part of the Declaration was the part we find least interesting—the long list of specific grievances which takes up exactly two-thirds of the document. It was also the least original part. By 1776 the colonists had accumulated a ready supply of these lists, and Jefferson borrowed freely from several of them.

Only the first 300 words of the Declaration make up the "immortal" part of it and these are more properly Jefferson's own. However, even here, as Jefferson himself said, all their "authority" rests on the "harmonizing sentiments of the day." To the student of eighteenth-century moral philosophy they are very resonant indeed. Virtually every phrase evokes long passages from celebrated philosophical works—"self-evident" truths, from John Locke and Thomas Reid; "all men are created equal," the mighty Linnean argument against all kinds of hereditary privilege; "inalienable rights," from Thomas Hutcheson; "the pursuit of happiness," Hutcheson again and Adam Smith; "deriving their just powers from the consent of the governed," the compact theory of John Locke. Into these two brief paragraphs the bookish Jefferson compressed whole volumes, and in doing so he tied a remote colonial rebellion to the highest hopes of the Atlantic world.

It is often said that the grievances enumerated in the Declaration were somewhat arbitrarily directed at the king because the colonists, having already repudiated the authority of Parliament over them, had no one else to declare their independence from. A careful reader of the Declaration will, however, detect a second villain in the piece—the British people. Jefferson had an idiosyncratic theory that Americans had become independent when they left Europe, and had voluntarily allied with the *people* of Great Britain, accepting with them a common sovereign. "We might have been a free and a great people together," Jefferson wrote in a part of his draft which Congress subsequently deleted. Instead "we must endeavor to forget our former love for them, and to hold them as we hold the rest of mankind enemies in war, in peace friends." Here Jefferson addressed, more forthrightly than the version Congress eventually approved, the national meaning of the dissolution of the "political bands" connecting "one people . . . with another."

On July 2, 1776, with Richard Henry Lee's motion before it, Congress formally voted the independence of the United States. For the next two days it debated and amended Jefferson's draft of the Declaration. Someone has counted more than eighty changes made in the text. Old Benjamin Franklin was kind enough to try to divert its fretful young author with a joke or two; even so, Jefferson felt his work had been "mangled." The amended version was adopted by Congress on July 4, promptly printed up, and "submitted to a candid world."

The Unanimous Declaration of the Thirteen United States of America

When in the Course of human events it becomes necessary for one people to dissolve the political bands which have connected them with another, and to assume among the Powers of the earth, the separate and equal station to which the Laws of Nature and of Nature's God entitle them, a decent respect to the opinions of mankind requires that they should declare the causes which impel them to the separation.[1]

---

[1]Paragraphing has been added according to that in Jefferson's draft.

We hold these truths to be self-evident, that all men are created equal, that they are endowed by their Creator with certain unalienable Rights, that among these are Life, Liberty and the pursuit of Happiness. That to secure these rights, Governments are instituted among Men, deriving their just Powers from the consent of the governed. That whenever any Form of Government becomes destructive of these ends, it is the Right of the People to alter or to abolish it, and to institute new Government, laying its foundation on such principles and organizing its Powers in such form, as to them shall seem most likely to effect their Safety and Happiness. Prudence, indeed, will dictate that Governments long established should not be changed for light and transient causes; and accordingly all experience hath shewn, that mankind are more disposed to suffer, while evils are sufferable, than to right themselves by abolishing the forms to which they are accustomed. But when a long train of abuses and usurpations, pursuing invariably the same Object evinces a design to reduce them under absolute Despotism, it is their right, it is their duty to throw off such Government, and to provide new Guards for their future security. Such has been the patient sufferance of these Colonies; and such is now the necessity which constrains them to alter their former Systems of Government. The history of the present King of Great Britain is a history of repeated injuries and usurpations, all having in direct object the establishment of an absolute Tyranny over these States. To prove this, let Facts be submitted to a candid world.

He has refused his Assent to Laws, the most wholesome and necessary for the public good.

He has forbidden his Governors to pass Laws of immediate and pressing importance, unless suspended in their operation till his Assent should be obtained; and when so suspended, he has utterly neglected to attend to them.

He has refused to pass other Laws for the accommodation of large districts of people, unless those people would relinquish the right of Representation in the Legislature, a right inestimable to them and formidable to tyrants only.

He has called together legislative bodies at places unusual, uncomfortable, and distant from the depository of their Public Records, for the sole Purpose of fatiguing them into compliance with his measures.

He has dissolved Representative Houses repeatedly, for opposing with manly firmness his invasions on the rights of the People.

He has refused for a long time, after such dissolutions, to cause others to be elected; whereby the Legislative Powers, incapable of

Annihilation, have returned to the People at large for their exercise; the State remaining in the mean time exposed to all the dangers of invasion from without, and convulsions within.

He has endeavoured to prevent the Population of these States; for that purpose obstructing the Laws for Naturalization of Foreigners; refusing to pass others to encourage their migration hither, and raising the conditions of new Appropriations of Lands.

He has obstructed the Administration of Justice, by refusing his Assent to Laws for establishing Judiciary Powers.

He has made Judges dependent on his Will alone, for the tenure of their offices, and the amount and payment of their salaries.

He has erected a multitude of New Offices, and sent hither swarms of Officers to harass our People, and eat out their substance.

He has kept among us, in times of peace, Standing Armies without the consent of our legislatures.

He has affected to render the Military independent of and superior to the Civil Power.

He has combined with others to subject us to a jurisdiction foreign to our constitution, and unacknowledged by our laws; giving his Assent to their Acts of pretended Legislation:

For Quartering large bodies of armed troops among us:

For protecting them, by a mock Trial, from Punishment for any Murders which they should commit on the Inhabitants of these States:

For cutting off our Trade with all parts of the world:

For imposing Taxes on us without our Consent:

For depriving us in many cases, of the benefits of Trial by Jury:

For transporting us beyond Seas to be tried for pretended offences:

For abolishing the free System of English Laws in a neighbouring Province, establishing therein an Arbitrary government, and enlarging its Boundaries so as to render it at once an example and fit instrument for introducing the same absolute rule into these Colonies:

For taking away our Charters, abolishing our most valuable Laws, and altering fundamentally the Forms of our Governments:

For suspending our own Legislatures, and declaring themselves invested with Power to legislate for us in all cases whatsoever.

He has abdicated Government here, by declaring us out of his Protection, and waging War against us.

He has plundered our seas, ravaged our Coasts, burnt our towns, and destroyed the lives of our people.

He is at this time transporting large Armies of foreign Mercenaries to compleat the works of death, desolation and tyranny, already begun with circumstances of Cruelty and perfidy scarcely paralleled in the most barbarous ages, and totally unworthy the Head of a civilized nation.

He has constrained our fellow Citizens taken Captive on the high Seas to bear Arms against their Country, to become the executioners of their friends and Brethren, or to fall themselves by their Hands.

He has excited domestic insurrections amongst us, and has endeavoured to bring on the inhabitants of our frontiers, the merciless Indian Savages, whose known rule of warfare, is an undistinguished destruction of all ages, sexes and conditions.

In every stage of these Oppressions We have Petitioned for Redress in the most humble terms: Our repeated Petitions have been answered only by repeated injury. A Prince, whose character is thus marked by every act which may define a Tyrant, is unfit to be the ruler of a free People.

Nor have We been wanting in attentions to our British brethren. We have warned them from time to time of attempts by their legislature to extend an unwarrantable jurisdiction over us. We have reminded them of the circumstances of our emigration and settlement here. We have appealed to their native justice and magnanimity, and we have conjured them by the ties of our common kindred to disavow these usurpations, which, would inevitably interrupt our connections and correspondence. They too have been deaf to the voice of justice and of consanguinity. We must, therefore, acquiesce in the necessity, which denounces our Separation, and hold them, as we hold the rest of mankind, Enemies in War, in Peace Friends.

We, therefore, the Representatives of the United States of America, in General Congress, Assembled, appealing to the Supreme Judge of the world for the rectitude of our intentions, do, in the Name, and by Authority of the good People of these Colonies, solemnly publish and declare, That these United Colonies are, and of Right ought to be FREE AND INDEPENDENT STATES; that they are Absolved from all Allegiance to the British Crown, and that all political connection between them and the State of Great Britain, is and ought to be totally dissolved; and that, as Free and Independent States, they have full Power to levy War, conclude Peace, contract

Alliances, establish Commerce, and to do all other Acts and Things which Independent States may of right do. And for the support of this Declaration, with a firm reliance on the protection of divine Providence, we mutually pledge to each other our Lives, our Fortunes and our sacred Honor.

❁ ❁ ❁

The Declaration of Independence did not, immediately at least, set the world on its ear. A leading student of the French Revolution reported after diligent search that the document never "had any particular influence in that country." English radicals also ignored it. More surprisingly, Americans themselves gave it scant attention until several decades later. Its eventual celebrity derived from the happenstance custom of marking the nation's birthday on July 4. John Adams tells us that when the first anniversary of independence rolled around on July 2, 1777, everybody forgot about it until it was too late to make arrangements. The third being spoken for, Congress delayed its celebration until the fourth, the anniversary of the Declaration. Even so, another student has found that few Fourth of July orators ever quoted the language of the Declaration and almost none its preamble.

Only in the years before the Civil War, when the proposition that all men were created equal became the subject of bitter controversy, did the Declaration assume, in the North, the stature of an American creed. Wisconsin in 1848 was the first state to include the language of Jefferson's preamble in its constitution. And Abraham Lincoln made it his mission to recall the nation to "that sentiment in the Declaration of Independence, which gave liberty not alone to the people of this country, but hope to all the world, for all future time." (See Volume 1, Section 5, Reading 3.)

Jefferson kept his original draft of the Declaration, often showing it to visitors at Monticello. It is now in the Library of Congress. Two weeks after the Declaration was adopted, Congress ordered a fair copy to be drawn on parchment and signed by the delegates, a business that stretched into August. This "engrossed" copy was kept for 135 years by the State Department. In 1924 it was encased in a great marble and bronze shrine and, carefully protected from light, heat, and humidity, put on public display. Jefferson, whose journal entry for the day the Declaration was adopted recorded four thermometer readings, would have found in these arrangements much to interest him.

2

❀ ❀ ❀

The American Constitution
1787

*W*hen the thirteen colonies declared that they were independent states in 1776, they were "united" only in the sense that military allies, before and since, have been united. The only "political bands" that tied them before 1776 were those that connected them individually with Great Britain. Consequently, for the first several years of hostilities, patriot troops fought for their states or, as Ethan Allen was said to have put it at the battle of Fort Ticonderoga, "in the name of the Great Jehovah and the Continental Congress."

In November 1777, the Continental Congress adopted a frame of government that more closely tied the states to one another, the Articles of Confederation. By no means did the Articles create a united nation. A confederacy is by definition a league of independent states from which, implicitly, a member state reserves the right and the power to resign. The Articles of Confederation ensured the independence and equality of each of its thirteen members by requiring a unanimous vote of the states to ratify any tax bill and also to amend this "first American constitution."

From the beginning (the Articles were finally ratified in 1781) nationally minded Americans were unhappy with mere confederation. Congress, the sole governing body, was often incapable of providing

THE AMERICAN CONSTITUTION, THE BILL OF RIGHTS, AMENDMENTS TO THE CONSTITUTION Reprinted from the fascimile of the original, engrossed copy in the National Archives.

George Washington with the financial support he needed to keep an army in the field. After independence and peace were established, it was next to impossible to levy a tax. One state delegation or another voted against practically every money bill introduced in Congress. Effective diplomacy was also difficult because, as the British mocked, it was too expensive to send thirteen ambassadors to North America. Congress was unable to settle even petty squabbles between states, such as an argument between Virginians and Marylanders over fishing rights in the Chesapeake Bay. And in 1786 and 1787, when a Revolutionary War veteran, Daniel Shays, led a march of rebellious farmers in western Massachusetts, leaders in that state and elsewhere lamented the fact that there was no national force that could be sent into the Bay State to restore order.

More than any other incident, it was Shays' Rebellion that inspired a series of meetings that led, in the summer of 1787, to a constitutional convention in Philadelphia. This assembly of fifty-five men was officially empowered only to consider amendments that might improve the Articles of Confederation. In fact (and as everyone knew), they immediately set the Articles aside and began writing a new frame of government from scratch. The assembly included so many distinguished leaders, including George Washington and Benjamin Franklin, that it was the focus of attention in the United States even though its meetings were held in secret.

More important than either Washington or Franklin in calling for the convention was Alexander Hamilton of New York. More important than any of them in actually designing the Constitution was James Madison of Virginia. Not yet forty, these young men, together with the other delegates, were nevertheless as expert and as profound in their knowledge of political philosophy and history as anyone in the world.

True to their revolutionary heritage, they were wary of opportunities for tyrants to establish themselves in the government. Thus, for example, they developed the famous concepts of "separation of powers" among executive, legislative, and judicial branches of the government; and "checks and balances," the fact that, among and within the three branches, the exercise of power depended on the concurrence of several arms of the government, not one alone. However, the "Founding Fathers" were not democrats. They were skeptical of democracy, believing that "the mob" was likely to act rashly in times of stress and create, out of a demagogic hero, a tyrant who would suppress the liberties of all.

Indeed, the new Constitution created a strong executive, the president, where there had been no executive at all in the Articles, and the electoral college ensured that there would be at least one "layer" of government between the president and a popular vote. Another momentous departure from Confederation government was the power of Congress to tax nationally. No combination of states in the minority, let alone a single state, could veto such action. In fact, Article I, Section 10, rendered the states almost impotent in economic matters. Internal taxation remained within the states' competence, but all national economic powers, including the regulation of foreign and interstate commerce, was reserved to Congress.

In September, 1787, the Constitutional Convention adjourned and most members returned to their states to urge ratification of the new frame of government. By its own rules, the Constitution would go into effect when nine of the thirteen ratified it. Politically conservative as the document may have been, this provision too was a veritable act of revolution. Under the existing government, the Confederation, unanimity of the states was required to amend, and surely to replace, the Articles.

We the People of the United States, in Order to form a more perfect Union, establish Justice, insure domestic Tranquility, provide for the common defence, promote the general Welfare, and secure the Blessings of Liberty to ourselves and our Posterity, do ordain and establish this Constitution for the United States of America.

Article. I.

Section. 1. All legislative Powers herein granted shall be vested in a Congress of the United States, which shall consist of a Senate and House of Representatives.

Section. 2. The House of Representatives shall be composed of Members chosen every second Year by the People of the several States, and the Electors in each State shall have the Qualifications requisite for Electors of the most numerous Branch of the State Legislature.

No Person shall be a Representative who shall not have attained to the Age of twenty five Years, and been seven Years a Citizen of the United States, and who shall not, when elected, be an Inhabitant of that State in which he shall be chosen.

Representatives and direct Taxes[1] shall be apportioned among the several States which may be included within this Union, according to their respective Numbers, which shall be determined by adding to the whole Number of free Persons, including those bound to

---

[1]Modified by the Sixteenth Amendment.

Service for a Term of Years, and excluding Indians not taxed, three fifths of all other Persons.[2] The actual Enumeration shall be made within three Years after the first Meeting of the Congress of the United States, and within every subsequent Term of ten Years, in such Manner as they shall by Law direct. The Number of Representatives shall not exceed one for every thirty Thousand, but each State shall have at least one Representative; and until such enumeration shall be made, the State of New Hampshire shall be entitled to chuse three; Massachusetts eight; Rhode Island and Providence Plantations one; Connecticut five; New York six; New Jersey four; Pennsylvania eight; Delaware one; Maryland six; Virginia ten; North Carolina five; South Carolina five; and Georgia three.

When vacancies happen in the Representation from any State, the Executive Authority thereof shall issue Writs of Election to fill such Vacancies.

The House of Representatives shall chuse their Speaker and other Officers; and shall have the sole Power of Impeachment.

Section. 3. The Senate of the United States shall be composed of two Senators from each State, chosen by the Legislature thereof, for six Years; and each Senator shall have one Vote.[3]

Immediately after they shall be assembled in Consequence of the first Election, they shall be divided as equally as may be into three Classes. The Seats of the Senators of the first Class shall be vacated at the Expiration of the second Year, of the second Class at the Expiration of the fourth Year, and of the third Class at the Expiration of the sixth Year, so that one third may be chosen every second Year; and if Vacancies happen by Resignation, or otherwise, during the Recess of the Legislature of any State, the Executive thereof may make temporary Appointments until the next Meeting of the Legislature, which shall then fill such Vacancies.[4]

No Person shall be a Senator who shall not have attained to the Age of thirty Years, and been nine Years a Citizen of the United States, and who shall not, when elected, be an Inhabitant of that State for which he shall be chosen.

The Vice President of the United States shall be President of the Senate, but shall have no Vote, unless they be equally divided.

The Senate shall chuse their other Officers, and also a Presi-

---

[2]Replaced by the Fourteenth Amendment.
[3]Superseded by the Seventeenth Amendment.
[4]Modified by the Seventeenth Amendment.

dent pro tempore, in the Absence of the Vice President, or when he shall exercise the Office of President of the United States.

The Senate shall have the sole Power to try all Impeachments. When sitting for that Purpose, they shall be on Oath or Affirmation. When the President of the United States is tried, the Chief Justice shall preside: And no Person shall be convicted without the Concurrence of two thirds of the Members present.

Judgment in Cases of Impeachment shall not extend further than to removal from Office, and disqualification to hold and enjoy any Office of honor, Trust or Profit under the United States: but the Party convicted shall nevertheless be liable and subject to Indictment, Trial, Judgment and Punishment, according to Law.

Section. 4. The Times, Places and Manner of holding Elections for Senators and Representatives, shall be prescribed in each State by the Legislature thereof, but the Congress may at any time by Law make or alter such Regulation, except as to the Places of chusing Senators.

The Congress shall assemble at least once in every Year, and such Meeting shall be on the first Monday in December, unless they shall by Law appoint a different Day.[5]

Section. 5. Each House shall be the Judge of the Elections, Returns and Qualifications of its own Members, and a Majority of each shall constitute a Quorum to do Business; but a smaller Number may adjourn from day to day, and may be authorized to compel the Attendance of absent Members, in such manner, and under such Penalties as each House may provide.

Each House may determine the Rules of its Proceedings, punish its Members for disorderly Behaviour, and, with the Concurrence of two thirds, expel a Member.

Each House shall keep a Journal of its Proceedings, and from time to time publish the same, excepting such Parts as may in their Judgment require Secrecy; and the Yeas and Nays of the Members of either House on any question shall, at the Desire of one fifth of those Present, be entered on the Journal.

Neither House, during the Session of Congress, shall, without the Consent of the other, adjourn for more than three days, nor to any other Place than that in which the two Houses shall be sitting.

Section. 6. The Senators and Representatives shall receive a Compensation for their Services, to be ascertained by Law, and paid out

---

[5]Superseded by the Twentieth Amendment.

of the Treasury of the United States. They shall in all Cases, except Treason, Felony and Breach of the Peace, be privileged from Arrest during their Attendance at the Session of their respective Houses, and in going to and returning from the same; and for any Speech or Debate in either House, they shall not be questioned in any other Place.

No Senator or Representative shall, during the Time for which he was elected, be appointed to any civil Office under the Authority of the United States, which shall have been created, or the Emoluments whereof shall have been encreased during such time; and no Person holding any Office under the United States, shall be a Member of either House during his Continuance in Office.

Section. 7. All Bills for raising Revenue shall originate in the House of Representatives; but the Senate may propose or concur with Amendments as on other bills.

Every Bill which shall have passed the House of Representatives and the Senate shall, before it become a Law, be presented to the President of the United States; If he approve he shall sign it, but if not he shall return it, with his Objections to that House in which it shall have originated, who shall enter the Objections at large on their Journal, and proceed to reconsider it. If after such Reconsideration two thirds of that House shall agree to pass the Bill, it shall be sent, together with the Objections, to the other House, by which it shall likewise be reconsidered, and if approved by two thirds of that House, it shall become a Law. But in all such Cases the Votes of both Houses shall be determined by Yeas and Nays, and the Names of the Persons voting for and against the Bill shall be entered on the Journal of each House respectively. If any Bill shall not be returned by the President within ten Days (Sundays excepted) after it shall have been presented to him, the Same shall be a Law, in Manner as if he had signed it, unless the Congress by their Adjournment prevent its Return, in which Case it shall not be a Law.

Every Order, Resolution, or Vote to which the Concurrence of the Senate and House of Representatives may be necessary (except on a question of Adjournment) shall be presented to the President of the United States; and before the Same shall take Effect, shall be approved by him, or being disapproved by him shall be repassed by two thirds of the Senate and House of Representatives, according to the rules and Limitations prescribed in the Case of a Bill.

Section. 8. The Congress shall have Power To Lay and collect Taxes, Duties, Imposts and Excises, to pay the Debts and provide for the common Defence and general Welfare of the United States; but all

Duties, Imposts and Excises shall be uniform throughout the United States;

To borrow Money on the credit of the United States;

To regulate Commerce with foreign Nations, and among the several States, and with the Indian Tribes;

To establish an uniform Rule of Naturalization, and uniform Laws on the subject of Bankruptcies throughout the United States;

To coin Money, regulate the Value thereof, and of foreign Coin, and fix the Standard of Weights and Measures;

To provide for the Punishment of counterfeiting the Securities and current Coin of the United States;

To establish Post Offices and post Roads;

To promote the Progress of Science and useful Arts, by securing for limited Times to Authors and Inventors the exclusive Right to their respective Writings and Discoveries;

To constitute Tribunals inferior to the Supreme Court;

To define and punish Piracies and Felonies committed on the high Seas, and Offences against the Law of Nations;

To declare War, grant Letters of Marque and Reprisal, and make Rules concerning Captures on Land and Water;

To raise and support Armies, but no Appropriation of Money to that Use shall be for a longer Term than two Years;

To provide and maintain a Navy;

To make Rules for the government and Regulation of the land and naval Forces;

To provide for calling forth the Militia to execute the Laws of the Union, suppress Insurrections and repel Invasions;

To provide for organizing, arming, and disciplining, the Militia, and for governing such Part of them as may be employed in the Service of the United States, reserving to the States respectively, the Appointment of the Officers, and the Authority of training the Militia according to the discipline prescribed by Congress;

To exercise exclusive Legislation in all Cases whatsoever, over such District (not exceeding ten Miles square) as may, by Cession of particular States, and the Acceptance of Congress, become the Seat of the Government of the United States, and to exercise like Authority over all Places purchased by the consent of the Legislature of the State in which the Same shall be, for the Erection of Forts, Magazines, Arsenals, dock-Yards, and other needful Buildings;—And

To make all Laws which shall be necessary and proper for carrying into Execution the foregoing Powers, and all other Powers vested by this Constitution in the Government of the United States, or in any Department or Officer thereof.

Section. 9. The Migration or Importation of such Persons as any of the States now existing shall think proper to admit, shall not be prohibited by the Congress prior to the Year one thousand eight hundred and eight, but a Tax or Duty may be imposed on such Importation, not exceeding ten dollars for each Person.

The Privilege of the Writ of Habeas Corpus shall not be suspended, unless when in Cases of Rebellion or Invasion the public Safety may require it.

No Bill of Attainder or ex post facto Law shall be passed.

No Capitation, or other direct, Tax shall be laid, unless in Proportion to the Census or Enumeration herein before directed to be taken.

No Tax or Duty shall be laid on Articles exported from any State.

No Preference shall be given by any Regulation of Commerce or Revenue to the Ports of one State over those of another: nor shall Vessels bound to, or from, one State, be obliged to enter, clear, or pay Duties in another.

No Money shall be drawn from the Treasury, but in Consequence of Appropriations made by Law, and a regular Statement and Account of the Receipts and Expenditures of all public Money shall be published from time to time.

No Title of Nobility shall be granted by the United States: And no Person holding any Office of Profit or Trust under them, shall, without the Consent of the Congress, accept of any present, Emolument, Office, or Title, of any kind whatever, from any King, Prince, or foreign State.

Section. 10. No State shall enter into any Treaty, Alliance, or Confederation; grant Letters of Marque and Reprisal; coin Money; emit bills of Credit; make any Thing but gold and silver Coin a Tender in Payment of Debts; pass any Bill of Attainder, ex post facto Law, or Law impairing the Obligation of Contracts, or grant any Title of Nobility.

No State shall, without the Consent of the Congress, lay any Imposts or Duties on Imports or Exports, except what may be absolutely necessary for executing its inspection Laws: and the net Produce of all Duties and Imposts, laid by any State on Imports or Exports, shall be for the Use of the Treasury of the United States; and all such Laws shall be subject to the Revision and Controul of the Congress.

No State shall, without the Consent of Congress, lay any Duty of Tonnage, keep Troops or Ships of War in time of peace, enter into any Agreement or Compact with another State, or with a foreign Power, or engage in War, unless actually invaded, or in such imminent Danger as will not admit of delay.

Article. II.

Section. 1. The executive Power shall be vested in a President of the United States of America. He shall hold his Office during the Term of four Years, and, together with the Vice President, chosen for the same Term, be elected, as follows:

Each State shall appoint, in such Manner as the Legislature thereof may direct, a Number of Electors, equal to the whole Number of Senators and Representatives to which the State may be entitled in the Congress: but no Senator or Representative, or Person holding an Office of Trust or Profit under the United States, shall be appointed an Elector.

The Electors shall meet in their respective States, and vote by Ballot for two Persons, of whom one at least shall not be an Inhabitant of the same State with themselves. And they shall make a List of all the Persons voted for, and of the Number of Votes for each; which List they shall sign and certify, and transmit sealed to the Seat of the Government of the United States, directed to the President of the Senate. The President of the Senate shall, in the Presence of the Senate and House of Representatives, open all the Certificates, and the Votes shall then be counted. The Person having the greatest Number of Votes shall be the President, if such Number be a Majority of the whole Number of Electors appointed; and if there be more than one who have such Majority, and have an equal Number of Votes, then the House of Representatives shall immediately chuse by Ballot one of them for President; and if no Person have a Majority, then from the five highest on the List the said House shall in like Manner chuse the President. But in chusing the President, the Votes shall be taken by States, the Representation from each State having one Vote; A quorum for this Purpose shall consist of a Member or Members from two thirds of the States, and a Majority of all the States shall be necessary to a Choice. In every Case, after the Choice of the President, the Person having the greatest Number of Votes of the Electors shall be the Vice President. But if there should remain two or more who have equal Votes, the Senate shall chuse from them by Ballot the Vice President.[6]

---

[6]Superseded by the Twelfth Amendment.

The Congress may determine the Time of chusing the Electors, and the Day on which they shall give their Votes; which Day shall be the same throughout the United States.

No Person except a natural born Citizen, or a Citizen of the United States, at the time of the Adoption of this Constitution, shall be eligible to the Office of President, neither shall any Person be eligible to that Office who shall not have attained to the Age of thirty five Years, and been fourteen Years a Resident within the United States.

In Case of the Removal of the President from Office, or of his Death, Resignation, or Inability to discharge the Powers and Duties of the said Office, the Same shall devolve on the Vice President, and the Congress may by Law provide for the Case of Removal, Death, Resignation or Inability, both of the President and Vice President, declaring what Officer shall then act as President, and such Officer shall act accordingly, until the Disability be removed, or a President shall be elected.[7]

The President shall, at stated Times, receive for his Services, a Compensation, which shall neither be encreased nor diminished during the Period for which he shall have been elected, and he shall not receive within that Period any other Emolument from the United States, or any of them.

Before he enter on the Execution of his Office, he shall take the following Oath or Affirmation:—"I do solemnly swear (or affirm) that I will faithfully execute the Office of President of the United States, and will to the best of my Ability, preserve, protect and defend the Constitution of the United States."

Section. 2. The President shall be Commander in Chief of the Army and Navy of the United States, and of the Militia of the several States, when called into the actual Service of the United States; he may require the Opinion, in writing, of the principle Officer in each of the executive Departments, upon any Subject relating to the Duties of their respective Offices, and he shall have Power to grant Reprieves and Pardons for Offences against the United States, except in cases of Impeachment.

He shall have Power, by and with the Advice and Consent of the Senate, to make Treaties, provided two thirds of the Senators present concur; and he shall nominate, and by and with the Advice and Consent of the Senate, shall appoint Ambassadors, other public Ministers and Consuls, Judges of the supreme Court, and all other

---

[7]Modified by the Twenty-fifth Amendment.

Officers of the United States, whose Appointments are not herein otherwise provided for, and which shall be established by Law; but the Congress may by Law vest the Appointment of such inferior Officers, as they think proper, in the President alone, in the Courts of Law, or in the Heads of Departments.

The President shall have Power to fill up all Vacancies that may happen during the Recess of the Senate, by granting Commissions which shall expire at the End of their next Session.

Section. 3. He shall from time to time give to the Congress Information of the State of the Union, and recommend to their Consideration such Measures as he shall judge necessary and expedient; he may, on extraordinary Occasions, convene both Houses, or either of them, and in Case of Disagreement between them, with Respect to the Time of Adjournment, he may adjourn them to such Time as he shall think proper; he shall receive Ambassadors and other public Ministers; he shall take Care that the Laws be faithfully executed, and shall Commission all the Officers of the United States.

Section. 4. the President, Vice President and all civil Officers of the United States, shall be removed from Office on Impeachment for, and Conviction of, Treason, Bribery, or other high Crimes and Misdemeanors.

Article. III.

Section. 1. The judicial Power of the United States, shall be vested in one supreme Court, and in such inferior Courts as the Congress may from time to time ordain and establish. The Judges, both of the supreme and inferior Courts, shall hold their Offices during good Behaviour, and shall, at stated Times, receive for their Services, a Compensation, which shall not be diminished during their Continuance in Office.

Section. 2. The judicial Power shall extend to all Cases, in Law and Equity, arising under this Constitution, the Laws of the United States, and Treaties made, or which shall be made, under their Authority;—to all Cases affecting Ambassadors, other public Ministers and Consuls;—to all Cases of admiralty and maritime Jurisdiction;—to Controversies to which the United States shall be a Party;—to Controversies between two or more States;—between a State and Citizens of another State;[8]—between Citizens of different States,—between Citizens of the same State claiming Lands under

---

[8]Modified by the Eleventh Amendment.

Grants of different States, and between a State, or the Citizens thereof, and foreign States, Citizens or Subjects.

In all Cases affecting Ambassadors, other public Ministers and Consuls, and those in which a State shall be Party, the supreme Court shall have original Jurisdiction. In all the other Cases before mentioned, the supreme Court shall have appellate Jurisdiction, both as to Law and Fact, with such Exceptions, and under such Regulations as the Congress shall make.

The Trial of all Crimes, except in Cases of Impeachment, shall be by Jury; and such Trial shall be held in the State where the said Crimes shall have been committed; but when not committed within any State, the trial shall be at such Place or Places as the Congress may by Law have directed.

Section. 3. Treason against the United States, shall consist only in levying War against them, or in adhering to their Enemies, giving them Aid and Comfort. No Person shall be convicted of Treason unless on the Testimony of two Witnesses to the same overt Act, or on Confession in open Court.

The Congress shall have power to declare the Punishment of Treason, but no Attainder of Treason shall work Corruption of Blood, or Forfeiture except during the Life of the Person attained.

Article. IV.

Section. 1. Full Faith and Credit shall be given in each State to the public Acts, Records, and judicial Proceedings of every other State. And the Congress may by general Laws prescribe the Manner in which such Acts, Records and Proceedings shall be proved, and the Effect thereof.

Section 2. The Citizens of each State shall be entitled to all Privileges and Immunities of Citizens in the several States.

A Person charged in any State with Treason, Felony, or other Crime, who shall flee from Justice, and be found in another State, shall on Demand of the executive Authority of the State from which he fled, be delivered up, to be removed to the State having Jurisdiction of the Crime.

No Person held to Service or Labour in one State, under the Laws thereof, escaping into another, shall, in Consequence of any Law or Regulation therein, be discharged from such Service or Labour, but shall be delivered up on Claim of the Party to whom such Service or Labour may be due.

Section. 3. New States may be admitted by the Congress into this Union; but no new State shall be formed or erected within the

Jurisdiction of any other State, nor any State be formed by the Junction of two or more States, or Parts of States, without the Consent of the Legislatures of the States concerned as well as of the Congress.

The Congress shall have Power to dispose of and make all needful Rules and Regulations respecting the Territory or other Property belonging to the United States; and nothing in this Constitution shall be so construed as to Prejudice any Claims of the United States, or of any particular State.

Section. 4. The United States shall guarantee to every State in this Union a Republican Form of Government, and shall protect each of them against Invasion; and on Application of the Legislature, or of the Executive (when the Legislature cannot be convened) against domestic Violence.

Article. V.

The Congress, whenever two thirds of both Houses shall deem it necessary, shall propose Amendments to this Constitution, or, on the Application of the Legislatures of two thirds of the several States, shall call a Convention for proposing Amendments, which, in either Case, shall be valid to all Intents and Purposes, as Part of this Constitution, when ratified by the Legislatures of three fourths of the several States, or by Conventions in three fourths thereof, as the one or the other Mode of Ratification may be proposed by the Congress; Provided that no Amendment which may be made prior to the Year One thousand eight hundred and eight shall in any Manner affect the first and fourth Clauses in the Ninth Section of the first Article; and that no State, without its Consent, shall be deprived of its equal Suffrage in the Senate.

Article. VI.

All Debts contracted and Engagements entered into, before the Adoption of this Constitution, shall be as valid against the United States under this Constitution, as under the Confederation.

This Constitution, and the Laws of the United States which shall be made in Pursuance thereof; and all Treaties made, or which shall be made, under the Authority of the United States, shall be the supreme Law of the Land; and the Judges in every State shall be bound thereby, any Thing in the Constitution or Laws of any State to the Contrary notwithstanding.

The Senators and Representatives before mentioned, and the

Members of the several State Legislatures, and all executive and judicial Officers, both of the United States and of the several States, shall be bound by Oath or Affirmation, to support this Constitution; but no religious Test shall ever be required as a Qualification to any Office or public Trust under the United States.

Article. VII.

The Ratification of the Conventions of nine States, shall be sufficient for the Establishment of this Constitution between the States so ratifying the Same.

done in Convention by the Unanimous Consent of the States present the Seventeenth Day of September in the Year of our Lord one thousand seven hundred and Eighty seven and of the Independence of the United States of America the Twelfth. *In witness* whereof We have hereunto subscribed our Names,

❖ ❖ ❖

If what the Founding Fathers did was revolutionary, the revolution was bloodless. By early 1789, eleven of the thirteen states, including all the large states, had ratified the Constitution. (See Volume 1, Section 2, Reading 5.) North Carolina held out until November, when a Bill of Rights was appended to the Constitution, and little Rhode Island, which, because of its size, feared domination by other states and prized independence of action, remained out of the Union until May 1790.

3

❖ ❖ ❖

The Bill of Rights
1789

*A*t one time, "liberty" meant *privilege*, a special exemption from restraints and restrictions that was granted to certain people. The liberties listed in the English *Magna Carta* of 1215, for example, applied only to the people of the baronial class with whom King John had been disputing. During medieval times, the inhabitants of cities were granted certain liberties not shared by other subjects of the kingdom. Sometimes monopolies and other economic privileges were called liberties. Examples of these liberties included the exclusive right of a baker's guild to set standards regarding the quality and quantity in the baking of bread and the price at which a loaf was sold, or the special privileges enjoyed within the British empire by the East India Company.

Colonial Americans were familiar with all three kinds of liberties. In some contexts, the American tobacco growers' monopoly on the English market was called a liberty. The residents of Connecticut and Rhode Island, corporate colonies until they gained independence, possessed, by virtue of their colonial charters, certain liberties not shared by the inhabitants of other colonies. However, what made being British very special to Britons and colonial Americans was the fact that, unlike people of other nationalities, all free British subjects possessed, because of a law that no lawmaker might alter, wide-ranging guarantees against arbitrary treatment by their rulers.

The personal liberties of *Magna Carta* had long since been extended from the nobility to all English freemen. When King James II was deposed in 1688, his successors, William and Mary, in return for their crowns, signed the 1689 English Bill of Rights, which also extended to Americans. What was special about liberties in the British empire was that they extended to all freemen, and they were no longer privileges but rights.

Indeed, Americans had fought the Revolution because they believed that the King and Parliament were attempting to abridge these rights. Consequently, when they wrote the constitutions of their independent states, nearly every colony included a bill of rights.

The absence of a bill of rights in the federal Constitution of 1787 was, in the minds of many Anti-Federalists, therefore an argument against ratifying it. Several states ratified the Constitution with the provisions or recommendation that a bill of rights be added to the document. North Carolina and Rhode Island remained aloof from the new Union until passage of a bill of rights was assured. In "Federalist No. 84," Alexander Hamilton argued that it was not necessary to include a bill of rights in the Constitution. He pointed out that Anti-Federalists in New York had never complained about the absence of a bill of rights from New York's Constitution. And that was how it should be, he said, for a specific tabulation of rights would have been superfluous. The individual's rights were implicit in or scattered about New York's constitution, and the federal constitution.

Other Federalists argued that a constitutional bill of rights was unnecessary because the states had already provided their own. Nevertheless, sentiment on behalf of a federal bill of rights was so strong that the first Congress adopted ten amendments to the Constitution in September 1789. They were ratified in December 1791.

Amendment I

Congress shall make no law respecting an establishment of religion, or prohibiting the free exercise thereof; or abridging the freedom of speech, or of the press; or the right of the people peaceably to assemble, and to petition the Government for a redress of grievances.

Amendment II

A well regulated Militia, being necessary to the security of a free State, the right of the people to keep and bear Arms shall not be infringed.

Amendment III

No Soldier shall, in time of peace, be quartered in any house, without the consent of the Owner, nor in time of war, but in a manner to be prescribed by law.

Amendment IV

The right of the people to be secure in their persons, houses, papers, and effects, against unreasonable searches and seizures, shall not be violated, and no Warrants shall issue, but upon probable cause, supported by Oath or affirmation, and particularly describing the place to be searched, and the persons or things to be seized.

Amendment V

No person shall be held to answer for a capital or otherwise infamous crime, unless on a presentment or indictment of a Grand Jury, except in cases arising in the land or naval forces, or in the Militia, when in actual service in time of War or public danger; nor shall any person be subject for the same offence to be twice put in jeopardy of life or limb; nor shall be compelled in any criminal case to be a witness against himself, nor be deprived of life, liberty, or property, without due process of law; nor shall private property be taken for public use, without just compensation.

Amendment VI

In all criminal prosecutions, the accused shall enjoy the right to a speedy and public trial, by an impartial jury of the State and district wherein the crime shall have been committed, which district shall have been previously ascertained by law, and to be informed of the nature and cause of the accusation; to be confronted with the witnesses against him; to have compulsory process for obtaining witnesses in his favor, and to have the Assistance of Counsel for his defence.

Amendment VII

In suits at common law, where the value in controversy shall exceed twenty dollars, the right of trial by jury shall be preserved, and no fact tried by a jury, shall be otherwise reexamined in any

Court of the United States, than according to the rules of the common law.

Amendment VIII

Excessive bail shall not be required, nor excessive fines imposed, nor cruel and unusual punishments inflicted.

Amendment IX

The enumeration in the Constitution, of certain rights, shall not be construed to deny or disparage others retained by the people.

Amendment X

The powers not delegated to the United States by the Constitution; nor prohibited by it to the States, are reserved to the States respectively, or to the people.

❖ ❖ ❖

For more than a hundred years, Americans had little doubt about what the Bill of Rights said. The brief amendments seemed crystal clear, their meaning established through centuries of precedent in England. Comparatively few cases testing the interpretation of them came before the Supreme Court. (By comparison, the Fourteenth Amendment was a snarl of interpretive difficulty from the beginning.)

In the second half of the twentieth century, however, many rights listed in the first ten amendments became the object of intensive scrutiny that, under the liberal Warren Court of 1953–1969, usually meant a vast broadening of their meaning. For example, the guarantees of freedom of speech and freedom of the press in the first amendment were extended to permit publication of pornography which previous generations of Americans had seen as no abridgement of liberty to prohibit. Curiously, Alexander Hamilton had argued against trying to specify freedom of the press as a right because of the snares he saw in attempting to interpret it: "What is the liberty of the press? Who could give it any definition which would not leave the utmost latitude for evasion? I hold it to be impracticable; and from this I infer, that its security, whatever fine declarations may be inserted in any constitution respecting it, must altogether depend on public opinion, and on the general spirit of the people and of the government."

The broad reinterpretation of the Bill of Rights in our own time, whether in allowing almost any kind of public expression, in making very specific the procedures that guarantee the rights of persons accused of crimes, or even in temporarily abolishing the death penalty under the "cruel and unusual punishments" provision of the eighth amendment, reflects well Hamilton's shrewd insight and the wisdom of the "Founding Fathers" in providing a clear means of amendment within the Constitution.

4

❖ ❖ ❖

Amendments to the Constitution
1795–1971

Americans have amended the
Constitution twenty-six times, or, on the average, about once every seven
years. However, the Bill of Rights was ratified so soon after the ratification
of the Constitution, and almost as a condition of ratification, that the first
ten amendments may reasonably be considered part and parcel of the
original document—in which case it can be said that the Constitution has
been amended only about once every twelve years.

Moreover, the most important amendments have come in two
bunches. These are the "Civil War Amendments" (the 13th, 14th,
and 15th), ratified between 1865 and 1870, and the "Progressive
Amendments" (the 16th, 17th, 18th, and 19th), ratified between 1913
and 1920.

One of these Progressive Amendments, the 18th—or Prohibition—
Amendment, which made it illegal to import, manufacture, sell, or
transport intoxicating liquors, was revoked by the 21st—or Repeal—
Amendment fourteen years after Prohibition went into effect. The 18th
is generally conceded to have been a colossal blunder. The Constitution is
intended to be a instrument of *basic* law, not a hodgepodge of ordinances to
be modified according to the opinion, mood, or whim of the people on a
very specific matter at a particular time. Only two "frivolous" amendments
over almost two hundred years is not a bad record. In fact, since 1789 more
than 6000 amendments have actually been proposed in Congress. Of these,
only thirty-three have been passed and sent to the states for ratification.

Amendment XVIII[1]

Section. 1. After one year from the ratification of this article the manufacture, sale, or transportation of intoxicating liquors within, the importation thereof into, or the exportation thereof from the United States and all territory subject to the jurisdiction thereof for beverage purposes is hereby prohibited.
Section. 2. The Congress and the several States shall have concurrent power to enforce this article by appropriate legislation.
Section. 3. This article shall be inoperative unless it shall have been ratified as an amendment to the Constitution by the legislatures of the several States, as provided in the Constitution, within seven years from the date of the submission hereof to the States by the Congress.

Amendment XXI[2]

Section. 1. The eighteenth article of amendment to the Constitution of the United States is hereby repealed.
Section. 2. The transportation or importation into any State, Territory, or possession of the United States for delivery or use therein of intoxicating liquors, in violation of the laws thereof, is hereby prohibited.
Section. 3. This article shall be inoperative unless it shall have been ratified as an amendment of the Constitution by conventions in the several States, as provided in the Constitution, within seven years from the date of the submission hereof to the States by the Congress.

❊ ❊ ❊

The 11th Amendment may also be passed over lightly. Enacted by Congress in 1794 and ratified the next year, it provides that no one may sue a state government in the federal courts. The 11th was inspired by the ruling of the Supreme Court in *Chisholm* v. *Georgia* that citizens and foreigners did indeed possess this right. It was ratified very quickly by state governments anxious to assure themselves of this exemption and is chiefly notable as an example of a "check" on the power of the Supreme Court. That is, just as the impeachment of existing Justices or

---

[1]Passed December 18, 1917. Ratified January 16, 1919.
[2]Passed February 20, 1933. Ratified December 5, 1933.

appointments of new Justices to the Court are "checks" (see Volume 2, Section 1, Reading 4), an unpopular Court interpretation of the Constitution may be "checked," or nullified, by Constitutional Amendment.

Amendment XI[1]

The Judicial power of the United States shall not be construed to extend to any suit in law or equity, commenced or prosecuted against one of the United States by Citizens of another State, or by Citizens or Subjects of any Foreign State.

❖ ❖ ❖

The Civil War/Civil Rights Amendments

*A*fter the ratification of the 12th Amendment in 1804, the Constitution was unchanged for sixty years. By 1864, however, the agony and turmoil of the Civil War, then near the end of its third year, dictated that at least one significant amendment was in order. By the end of 1864, it was clear to all, including Confederate leaders who did not delude themselves, that American Negro slavery was dead. By 1865, even Jefferson Davis was prevailed upon to pledge manumission for slaves who donned Confederate gray. In the North, opposition to abolition virtually ceased to exist. When Congress approved the 13th Amendment on January 31, 1865, only a handful of men voted nay. In less than a year, the amendment was ratified.

It was soon clear, however, that neither President Andrew Johnson, the courts, nor many of the whites of both the South and North regarded freedom as tantamount to citizenship. Southern state governments set up with Johnson's approval wrote the "Black Codes" which gave a decidedly inferior status to the freedmen. In several northern states, laws preventing blacks from voting were reinstituted or reaffirmed. Such discrimination was all quite constitutional. Defining citizenship was, in 1866, clearly the prerogative of individual state governments.

The Radical Republicans, who won control of Reconstruction policy after the Congressional elections of 1866, were determined that full

---

[1]Passed March 4, 1794. Ratified January 23, 1795.

citizenship be accorded to the freedmen. Even extreme idealists like Thaddeus Stevens had earlier expressed their reluctant willingness to allow discrimination against blacks in the North, but there was no way, under the Constitution, that full citizenship could be accorded in some states and not in others. So, the 14th Amendment forbade all states from abridging the rights of or denying equal legal protection to any United States citizen.

There were exceptions, detailed in Section 3 of the amendment. For example, Confederates who had earlier taken an oath of loyalty to the Constitution of the United States were to be deprived of their civil rights until pardoned by Congress. Also, Section 4 forbade the repayment of Confederate debts.

The 15th Amendment forbade states to deny the right to vote to anyone on the basis of race, color, or previous condition of servitude—in other words, the former slaves. It was adopted by Congress shortly after the presidential election of 1868 when a careful analysis of the results showed that, even this soon after the Civil War, the Republican candidate Ulysses S. Grant might not have won except for the almost solid support of southern blacks. Had blacks been able to vote in several northern states, Grant's plurality would not have been so slender in the North. The Republicans had no intention of yielding control of the federal government to the Democrats, whom they associated with treason, so soon after the dreadful war. The 15th Amendment, while surely motivated by idealism as well, was very much motivated by the political situation in 1869.

Amendment XIII[1]

Section. 1. Neither slavery nor involuntary servitude, except as a punishment for crime whereof the party shall have been duly convicted, shall exist within the United States, or any place subject to their jurisdiction.

Section. 2. Congress shall have power to enforce this article by appropriate legislation.

Amendment XIV[2]

Section. 1. All persons born or naturalized in the United States, and subject to the jurisdiction thereof, are citizens of the United States and of the State wherein they reside. No State shall make or enforce any law which shall abridge the privileges or immunities of citizens

---

[1]Passed January 31, 1865. Ratified December 6, 1865.
[2]Passed June 13, 1866. Ratified July 9, 1865.

of the United States; nor shall any State deprive any person of life, liberty, or property, without due process of law; nor deny to any person within its jurisdiction the equal protection of the laws.

Section. 2. Representatives shall be apportioned among the several States according to their respective numbers, counting the whole number of persons in each State, excluding Indians not taxed. But when the right to vote at any election for the choice of electors for President and Vice-President of the United States, Representatives in Congress, the Executive and Judicial officers of a State, or the members of the Legislature thereof, is denied to any of the male inhabitants of such State, being twenty-one years of age, and citizens of the United States, or in any way abridged, except for participation in rebellion, or other crime, the basis of representation therein shall be reduced in the proportion which the number of such male citizens shall bear to the whole number of male citizens twenty-one years of age in such State.

Section. 3. No person shall be a Senator or Representative in Congress, or elector of President and Vice-President, or hold any office, civil or military, under the United States, or under any State, who, having previously taken an oath, as a member of Congress, or as an officer of the United States, or as a member of any State legislature, or as an executive or judicial officer of any State, to support the Constitution of the United States, shall have engaged in insurrection or rebellion against the same, or given aid or comfort to the enemies thereof. But Congress may by a vote of two-thirds of each House, remove such disability.

Section. 4. The validity of the public debt of the United States, authorized by law, including debts incurred for payment of pensions and bounties for services in suppressing insurrection or rebellion, shall not be questioned. But neither the United States nor any State shall assume or pay any debt or obligation incurred in aid of insurrection or rebellion against the United States, or any claim for the loss or emancipation of any slave; but all such debts, obligations, and claims shall be held illegal and void.

Section. 5. The Congress shall have the power to enforce, by appropriate legislation, the provisions of this article.

Amendment XV[3]

Section. 1. The right of citizens of the United States to vote shall not be denied or abridged by the United States or by any State on

---

[3]Passed February 26, 1869. Ratified February 2, 1870.

account of race, color, or previous condition of servitude—
Section. 2. The Congress shall have power to enforce this article by appropriate legislation.

With the end of Reconstruction in 1877, the 15th Amendment was effectively allowed to lapse in the southern states. At first, through terrorism of the Ku Klux Klan and then through economic pressures (most blacks were tenant farmers, dependent on landowners for their living), blacks were informally disenfranchised. They were kept from voting in a number of legal ways. For example, requiring voters to pass a literacy test did not deny anyone's right to vote on the basis of race, color, or previous condition of servitude, but when administered by local officials it could easily serve that purpose. Simpler tests were given to whites, or grading was done on a double standard. Charging would-be voters a "poll tax," a fairly substantial sum, disqualified many blacks, to whom a few dollars could mean the difference between hunger and minimal comfort. "Grandfather clauses" in some states' electoral laws provided that people whose grandfathers had been eligible to vote were exempted from literacy tests and poll taxes. These contrivances, strictly construed, were not in violation of the 15th Amendment, but they kept blacks away from the polls. No black man's grandfather had been eligible to vote during his lifetime.

Such palpable evasion of the spirit of the 15th Amendment was possible only with the connivance of the courts. The Supreme Court's decision in the case of *Plessy* v. *Ferguson* in 1896 (see Volume 2, Section 2, Reading 4) was a signal to white southern racists that they could evade the Civil War Amendments with impunity. Not until the 1940s and 1950s did the courts begin to enforce the 14th and 15th Amendments with any consistency. One historian has correctly described the Civil War Amendments as the nation's "deferred commitment" to its black citizens. In fact, it required another constitutional amendment, the 24th, ratified in 1964, to eliminate the poll tax as a means of disenfranchising the poor, whatever their race.

Amendment XXIV[1]

Section. 1. The right of citizens of the United States to vote in any primary or other election for President or Vice President, or for Senator or Representative in Congress, shall not be denied or

---

[1]Passed August 27, 1962. Ratified January 23, 1964.

abridged by the United States or any State by reason of failure to pay any poll tax or other tax.

Section. 2. The Congress shall have power to enforce this article by appropriate legislation.

❖ ❖ ❖

The Progressive Amendments

The so-called "progressive movement" was in reality a mélange of reform impulses that swept the country during the first two decades of the twentieth century, some of them quite in conflict with others. Nevertheless, the demand for change was real and formidable and resulted in the ratification of four amendments within six years.

The Prohibition Amendment, the 18th, has already been noted. The 16th, ratified in 1913, made a graduated income tax constitutional. Previously, as the Supreme Court ruled in 1895, Congress could not levy a direct tax on individuals because it would mean taxing different states at different rates. The Constitution required that direct taxes be apportioned equally among the states, that is, at a rate proportionate to a state's population. However, the income tax was based on wealth. For example, in 1890 Alabama had a greater population than New Jersey but the per capita income of New Jersey was double and perhaps as much as triple that of Alabama. This meant that a federal income tax would raise at least two times as much in New Jersey as in Alabama—a situation which was not constitutional. Thus, the 16th Amendment became the basis of our income tax today.

The 17th Amendment removed the power to elect United States Senators from the state legislatures and required that senators be elected by popular vote. This amendment marked one of the most significant philosophical departures from the intentions of the Founding Fathers. They had put election of senators in the hands of state legislators deliberately and explicitly to remove senators a step from "the democracy," the people. One of the underlying beliefs of many progressives was that the more democracy there was in government, the less likely it was that government would be corrupt and beholden to special interests.

Any number of similarly democratic amendments were proposed during the progressive years, and their objects—the recall and the referendum—were enacted in many states. At the constitutional level, however, only the direct election of senators was enacted. One of the progressive proposals is still periodically proposed in Congress: the abolition of the electoral college and the direct popular election of the president. The electoral college too was seen by the Founding Fathers as a device to remove the president several steps from direct democracy.

The 19th Amendment prohibits states from denying citizens the right to vote on the basis of their sex. It is commonly known as the Woman Suffrage Amendment.

Amendment XVI[1]

The Congress shall have power to lay and collect taxes on incomes, from whatever source derived, without apportionment among the several States, and without regard to any census or enumeration.

Amendment XVII[2]

The Senate of the United States shall be composed of two Senators from each State, elected by the people thereof, for six years; and each Senator shall have one vote. The electors in each State shall have the qualifications requisite for electors of the most numerous branch of the State legislature.

When vacancies happen in the representation of any State in the Senate, the executive authority of such State shall issue writs of election to fill such vacancies: *Provided*, That the legislature of any State may empower the executive thereof to make temporary appointments until the people fill the vacancies by election as the legislature may direct.

This amendment shall not be so construed as to affect the election or term of any Senator chosen before it becomes valid as part of the Constitution.

Amendment XIX[3]

The right of citizens of the United States to vote shall not be denied or abridged by the United States or by any State on account of sex.

---

[1]Passed July 12, 1909. Ratified February 3, 1913.

[2]Passed May 13, 1912. Ratified April 8, 1913.

[3]Passed June 4, 1919. Ratified August 18, 1920.

Congress shall have power to enforce this article by appropriate legislation.

In 1972, Congress approved another feminist amendment, the ERA or Equal Rights Amendment, which read: "Equality of rights under the law shall not be denied or abridged by the United States or by any State on account of sex." At first, the ERA sailed through almost enough state legislatures to be incorporated into the Constitution. But anti-ERA forces mobilized and ended the trend toward ratification. By 1979, the deadline for ratification, ERA was still three votes short of acceptance. In the meantime, Congress extended the cut-off date to June 30, 1982.

When three states rescinded their ratification, there was some question as to whether or not these reversals were constitutional. Anti-ERA forces argued they were, because of the unprecedented action of Congress in modifying the terms of ratification. In any case the issue was moot because ERA failed to win the approval of a single additional state during the three-year extension.

To date, therefore, the final amendment to the Constitution is the 26th, which extends the right to vote to all citizens over the age of eighteen. It has been called the "Baby Boom Amendment." Ratified with extraordinary haste in 1971, it was designed to appeal to the huge baby boom generation who were then reaching their maturity and who had been a source of considerable social tumult during the 1960s. Ironically, no sooner was the amendment ratified than the apparently intense interest of youth in politics evaporated. Statistically, the 18- to 21-year-old age group is by far the least likely to participate in or even express an interest in political issues and the right to vote.

Amendment XXVI[1]

Section. 1. The right of citizens of the United States, who are eighteen years of age or older, to vote shall not be denied or abridged by the United States or by any State on account of age.
Section. 2. The Congress shall have power to enforce this article by appropriate legislation.

[1]Passed March 23, 1971. Ratified July 5, 1971.

The Presidential Amendments

*T*he 12th, 20th, 22nd, 23rd, and 25th Amendments deal with presidential elections, terms, and succession. Each has its roots in specific historical circumstances.

The 12th Amendment, ratified in 1804, was written to ensure that the events of the election of 1800 would not be repeated. The Founding Fathers had assumed that the United States would be home to no political parties. Therefore, they reasoned, every four years the Electoral College would select the nation's best qualified person to be president. Because the vice-president succeeded to the presidency in case of a vacancy, it was assumed that the vice-president should be the second best qualified person. So, under the original Constitution, the person receiving the most electoral votes became president, the person receiving the second most vice-president.

Already in 1796, the inadequacy of the scheme in an age of political parties was made clear. Federalist John Adams and Republican Thomas Jefferson, representing different parties and running against one another, received, respectively, 71 and 68 electoral votes, with the intended Federalist vice-presidential candidate, Thomas Pinckney, running third with 59 votes. Adams' vice-president was, therefore, his chief political rival, Thomas Jefferson. Had Adams died in office, the representative of the opposition would have become president, not exactly what the Founding Fathers had in mind.

Adams did not die in office. Instead, in 1800 he was roundly defeated by the Republican ticket of Jefferson and Aaron Burr. However, no Republican elector was assigned to "throw away" a Burr vote so that Jefferson would have a majority. Instead, the two were locked in an electoral college draw. When that happens (and this is still the case), the power to break the tie goes to the House of Representatives. Finally, in 1801, the House chose Jefferson and he moved into the Executive Mansion. But he and his party were determined that the colossal snafu would not occur again. Their 12th Amendment required electors to distinguish their votes for president from their votes for vice-president.

The 20th Amendment changed Inauguration Day from March 4th to January 20th. Ratified in 1933, this amendment in part represented a recognition of the transportation and communications revolution of the nineteenth and twentieth centuries. It was no longer necessary to allow a president-elect four months to prepare for the presidency and travel to the national capital. The long interregnum seemed even longer in 1933 because the country was entrapped in the greatest crisis since the Civil War, the Great Depression. In November 1932, the electorate emphatically voted against the incumbent, Herbert C. Hoover, who was perceived as paralyzed by the economic disaster, and voted in the Democratic candidate, Franklin D. Roosevelt. Because the depression had assumed the character of an emergency, Hoover's four remaining months in office seemed like an eternity. The 20th amendment assured that there would not again be such an interminable period of "lame-duck" government.

The 22nd Amendment was inspired by FDR's historic presidency. Elected to the office four times, Roosevelt was so much a symbol of Republican disarray that in 1947 they used their control of Congress to draft an amendment to ensure that no future president would serve more terms than the two established as traditional by Washington, Jefferson, Madison, Monroe, and Jackson. Harry S. Truman, president in 1947, was exempted from the 22nd Amendment but wisely chose not to stand for re-election in 1952 when his second term ended. He would surely have been defeated.

By 1960, a majority of the population of Washington, D. C., was black, and the decision taken years before—that the District would not be self-governing—had become a civil rights question. This was the rationale for the 23rd Amendment, ratified in 1961, which enfranchises the residents of the District of Columbia in presidential elections. Previously, citizens of the District were not permitted to select Electoral College representatives.

The 25th Amendment enables the president to appoint a vice-president when there is a vacancy in the vice-presidency. As of 1965, this had happened twelve times—seven times when a president died in office and the vice-president assumed the position, and five times when the vice-president died in office, or, in the case of John C. Calhoun, resigned. At those various times, either the Secretary of State or the Speaker of the House of Representatives was next in line of succession. However, this state of affairs presented somewhat the same situation as had held between 1797 and 1801, when the president and vice-president represented different political parties. During those years, had an "accident of history"—the death of the president—occurred, the administration would have fallen to the political opposition. Likewise, were the vice-presidency vacant and the House of Representatives under the control of the opposition when the president died or resigned, the executive would change parties despite the fact that no such wish had been expressed by the electorate. Thus, the 25th Amendment, while giving the president substantial power to choose a successor, is actually a further reinforcement of our nation's principle of rule by majority.

Amendment XII[1]

The Electors shall meet in their respective States and vote by ballot for President and Vice-President, one of whom, at least, shall not be an inhabitant of the same State with themselves; they shall

---

[1]Passed December 9, 1803. Ratified June 15, 1804.

name in their ballots the person voted for as President, and in distinct ballots the person voted for as Vice-President, and they shall make distinct lists of all persons voted for as President, and of all persons voted for as Vice-President, and of the number of votes for each, which lists they shall sign and certify, and transmit sealed to the seat of the government of the United States, directed to the President of the Senate;—The President of the Senate shall, in the presence of the Senate and House of Representatives, open all the certificates and the votes shall then be counted;—The person having the greatest number of votes for President, shall be the President, if such number is a majority of the whole number of Electors appointed; and if no person have such majority, then from the persons having the highest numbers not exceeding three on the list of those voted for as President, the House of Representatives shall choose immediately, by ballot, the President. But in choosing the President, the votes shall be taken by states, the representation from each state having one vote; a quorum for this purpose shall consist of a member or members from two-thirds of the states, and a majority of all the states shall be necessary to a choice. And if the House of Representatives shall not choose a President whenever the right of choice shall devolve upon them, before the fourth day of March next following, then the Vice-President shall act as President, as in the case of the death or other constitutional disability of the President.—The person having the greatest number of votes as Vice-President, shall be the Vice-President, if such number be a majority of the whole number of Electors appointed, and if no person have a majority, then from the two highest numbers on the list, the Senate shall choose the Vice-President; a quorum for the purpose shall consist of two-thirds of the whole number of Senators, and a majority of the whole number shall be necessary to a choice. But no person constitutionally ineligible to the office of President shall be eligible to that of Vice-President of the United States.

Amendment XX[2]

Section. 1. The terms of the President and Vice-President shall end at noon on the 20th day of January, and the terms of Senators and Representatives at noon on the 3d day of January, of the years in which such terms would have ended if this article had not been ratified; and the terms of their successors shall then begin.

---

[2]Passed March 2, 1932. Ratified January 23, 1933.

Section. 2. The Congress shall assemble at least once in every year, and such meeting shall begin at noon on the 3d day of January, unless they shall by law appoint a different day.

Section. 3. If, at the time fixed for the beginning of the term of the President, the President elect shall have died, the Vice-President elect shall become President. If a President shall not have been chosen before the time fixed for the beginning of his term, or if the President elect shall have failed to qualify, then the Vice-President elect shall act as President until a President shall have qualified; and the Congress may by law provide for the case wherein neither a President elect nor a Vice-President elect shall have qualified, declaring who shall then act as President, or the manner in which one who is to act shall be selected, and such person shall act accordingly until a President or Vice-President shall have qualified.

Section. 4. The Congress may by law provide for the case of the death of any of the persons from whom the House of Representatives may choose a President whenever the right of choice shall have devolved upon them, and for the case of the death of any of the persons from whom the Senate may choose a Vice-President whenever the right of choice shall have devolved upon them.

Section. 5. Sections 1 and 2 shall take effect on the 15th day of October following the ratification of this article.

Section. 6. This article shall be inoperative unless it shall have been ratified as an amendment to the Constitution by the legislatures of three-fourths of the several States within seven years from the date of its submission.

Amendment XXII[3]

No person shall be elected to the office of the President more than twice, and no person who has held the office of President, or acted as President, for more than two years of a term to which some other person was elected President shall be elected to the office of the President more than once.

But this Article shall not apply to any person holding the office of President when this Article was proposed by the Congress, and shall not prevent any person who may be holding the office of President, or acting as President, during the term within which this Article becomes operative from holding the office of President or acting as President during the remainder of such term.

---

[3]Passed March 12, 1947. Ratified March 1, 1951.

Amendment XXIII[4]

Section. 1. The district constituting the seat of Government of the United States shall appoint in such manner as the Congress may direct:

A number of electors of President and Vice President equal to the whole number of Senators and Representatives in Congress to which the District would be entitled if it were a State, but in no event more than the least populous State; they shall be in addition to those appointed by the States, but they shall be considered, for the purposes of the election of President and Vice President, to be electors appointed by the State; and they shall meet in the District and perform such duties as provided by the twelfth article of amendment.

Section. 2. The Congress shall have power to enforce this article by appropriate legislation.

Amendment XXV[5]

Section. 1. In case of the removal of the President from office or of his death or resignation, the Vice President shall become President.

Section. 2. Whenever there is a vacancy in the office of the Vice President, the President shall nominate a Vice President who shall take office upon confirmation by a majority vote of both Houses of Congress.

Section. 3. Whenever the President transmits to the President pro tempore of the Senate and the Speaker of the House of Representatives his written declaration that he is unable to discharge the powers and duties of his office, and until he transmits to them a written declaration to the contrary, such powers and duties shall be discharged by the Vice President as Acting President.

Section. 4. Whenever the Vice President and a majority of either the principal officers of the executive department or of such other body as Congress may by law provide, transmit to the President pro tempore of the Senate and the Speaker of the House of Representatives their written declaration that the President is unable to discharge the powers and duties of his office, the Vice President shall immediately assume the powers and duties of the office of Acting President.

Thereafter, when the President transmits to the President pro

---

[4]Passed June 16, 1960. Ratified April 3, 1961.
[5]Passed July 6, 1965. Ratified February 11, 1967.

tempore of the Senate and the Speaker of the House of Representatives his written declaration that no inability exists, he shall resume the powers and duties of his office unless the Vice President and a majority of either the principal officers of the executive department or of such other body as Congress may by law provide, transmit within four days to the President pro tempore of the Senate and the Speaker of the House of Representatives their written declaration that the President is unable to discharge the powers and duties of his office. Thereupon Congress shall decide the issue, assembling within forty-eight hours for that purpose if not in session. If the Congress, within twenty-one days after receipt of the latter written declaration, or, if Congress is not in session, within twenty-one days after Congress is required to assemble, determines by two-thirds vote of both Houses that the President is unable to discharge the powers and duties of his office, the Vice President shall continue to discharge the same as Acting President; otherwise, the President shall resume the powers and duties of his office.

The 25th Amendment was called upon under the first president elected after its ratification. Republican Richard M. Nixon was elected president in 1968 and re-elected in 1972. In October 1973, under fire for taking bribes while governor of Maryland, Vice-president Spiro T. Agnew was forced to resign. Less than a year later, President Nixon himself resigned as a result of the "Watergate" scandal. Had the 25th Amendment not been in effect, Thomas P. "Tip" O'Neill, the Democratic Speaker of the House, would have become president, representing a major switch of parties and political philosophies. However, under the terms of the 25th Amendment, President Nixon had named as vice-president a member of his own party, Gerald Ford of Michigan. Curiously, when Ford named Nelson A. Rockefeller as vice-president, the two highest offices in the land were held by people who had never even stood as candidates in a national election.